Praise for the first edition

"If you ever thought that ecc
gripping drama, try reading this book."
— Khurram Husain, *Dawn*

"Masood covers decades of challenges to GDP conventions that make for a fascinating institutional and human story."
— Diane Coyle, *Nature*

"Masood's highly readable book is a useful reminder of what GDP is and what it isn't."
— N. Gregory Mankiw, *Science*

"Ehsan Masood unveils the genesis of GDP and how it shaped the modern economic paradigm. It comes at a time when a growing number of people are questioning this flawed metric."
— *Down to Earth*

"Fascinating. Whether happiness should be embedded into decisions on the economy is an important one, and whether GDP should be abandoned in favor of something better is too. Masood's book helps raise those questions and others in a thought provoking manner. That's much needed in every endeavor these days, and needed in few places more than in the economics profession."
— Simon Constable, *Forbes*

"In lively prose, Masood argues that GDP is flawed because it ignores volunteering, housework, environmental degradation, job satisfaction, and income inequality."
— *Kirkus Reviews*

GDP

The World's Most Powerful Formula and Why it Must Now Change

EHSAN MASOOD

ICON

Originally published in the United States in 2016 as *The Great Invention*,
published by Pegasus Books Ltd, 80 Broad St., 5th Floor, New York, NY 10004

Published in the UK in 2021
by Icon Books Ltd, Omnibus Business Centre,
39–41 North Road, London N7 9DP
email: info@iconbooks.com
www.iconbooks.com

Sold in the UK, Europe and Asia
by Faber & Faber Ltd, Bloomsbury House,
74–77 Great Russell Street,
London WC1B 3DA or their agents

Distributed in the UK, Europe and Asia
by Grantham Book Services, Trent Road, Grantham NG31 7XQ

Distributed in the USA
by Publishers Group West,
1700 Fourth Street, Berkeley, CA 94710

Distributed in Australia and New Zealand
by Allen & Unwin Pty Ltd,
PO Box 8500, 83 Alexander Street,
Crows Nest, NSW 2065

Distributed in South Africa
by Jonathan Ball, Office B4, The District,
41 Sir Lowry Road, Woodstock 7925

Distributed in India by Penguin Books India,
7th Floor, Infinity Tower – C, DLF Cyber City,
Gurgaon 122002, Haryana

Distributed in Canada by Publishers Group Canada,
76 Stafford Street, Unit 300
Toronto, Ontario M6J 2S1

ISBN: 978-178578-711-9

Text copyright © 2016, 2021 Ehsan Masood

The author has asserted his moral rights.

Interior design by Maria Fernandez

Printed and bound in Great Britain
by Clays Ltd, Elcograf S.p.A.

In memory of
Mahbub ul Haq
(1934–1998)

Ehsan Masood is a science journalist and senior editor at the journal *Nature*. A former Knight Science Journalism Fellow at the Massachusetts Institute of Technology, he has written and presented documentary programmes for BBC Radio 4. His previous books include *Science and Islam: A History* (Icon, 2017).

Contents

PREFACE TO THE SECOND EDITION

T he world of 2021 seems barely recognizable from 2016 when the first edition of this book (under its original title *The Great Invention*), was published in the United States.

As I write this (at the start of 2021), the coronavirus pandemic has taken close to 2 million lives and infected nearly 100 million people, and continues to decimate economies. Most of the world, with the exception of East Asia, is in some form of lockdown. Hundreds of millions, especially the lowest-paid workers in service industries, have become jobless. City-center offices lie empty. Hospitals are struggling to cope. Children are forced to stay at home while schools remain closed.

Although vaccines have arrived, it will take at least two years to vaccinate the world. In the meantime, the International Monetary Fund estimates a fall in global Gross Domestic Product (GDP) of more than 4 percent during 2020,[1] a level of drop not seen for at least a century. So many of the gains that have been made in lifting the poorest out of poverty stand at risk of being wiped out.

GDP is a count of a nation's economic activity. It is calculated by a country's national statistical office and includes what consumers spend in the shops, and what businesses and governments invest. GDP is a highly technical process, but eagerly anticipated and followed by a much wider group of non-specialists, including politicians and the public, along with economists, financial analysts, fund managers, and the media. The quarterly announcement of the latest data ranks as one of the great rituals of modern economic and political life. If GDP is more than in the previous three months, governments breathe a sigh of relief, but if GDP drops, or if even if it stays the same, the result can, potentially, be terminal for whoever is in power.

With economies in freefall, that is the pressure every government is now under. To boost economic activity—and therefore GDP—many countries' leaders have turned to the 1940s playbook of the English economist John Maynard Keynes (see Chapter 2). Business investment tends to be low during an economic downturn, so Keynes recommended a boost to government investment in such times to take up some of the slack. The ambition was to protect existing jobs where possible, and invest in big capital-intensive projects to create new ones. That is what countries are doing, in the expectation that doing so will create higher growth as measured by GDP.[2]

But there are important differences between today's world and that of Keynes. Today's industrial development must be weighed against environmental costs. The industrialization of the past few centuries has pumped enough carbon dioxide into the atmosphere to put the world on track to dangerous global warming. At the same time, a sixth mass extinction[3] is becoming more likely as humans continue to encroach into nature to build more homes, new railways, and entire new cities—simultaneously increasing the risks of zoonotic diseases such as COVID-19.[4]

All of this means that economic recovery needs to be greener if climate change, biodiversity loss and future pandemics are to be avoided. But the problem with measuring economic activity using GDP is that it rewards traditional, fossil fuel-powered economic development. In contrast, greener development takes longer and cannot be achieved in the time it takes for governments to sanction what are called 'shovel-ready' projects that can deliver faster growth. Faced with this choice, most governments are opting for the more traditional route: roads, housing developments, airports are all being green-lighted, regardless of whether the means to achieve development are credible, or sustainable.

Researchers increasingly are questioning whether GDP is fit for purpose: if the world is at risk of ecological grief, why are we still following its formula, they rightly ask.

In *The Value of Everything*, Mariana Mazzucato of University College London illustrates how GDP incentivizes those economic sectors that will push the index ever higher, regardless of whether they are causing planetary harm, or widening inequality.

Meanwhile, Diane Coyle of the University of Cambridge and Benjamin Mitra-Kahn of Australia's Intellectual Property Office have a two-step proposal. Firstly, to amend GDP by incorporating what it currently undervalues[5] and then to move away from using GDP and instead valuing different kinds of "capital," including human capital and natural capital as well as financial capital.[6]

A joint US–China team of researchers—Zhiyun Ouyang of the Chinese Academy of Sciences, Gretchen Daily of Stanford

University, and Jack Liu of Michigan State University—have been involved in implementing a concept they call Gross Ecosystem Product,[7] in which the value of the natural world is quantified in dollars and cents, so that the world knows what it is losing each time something like a forest or a wetland is cleared to make way for industrial activity. Even the venerable *Financial Times* of London recently weighed in with an editorial calling for a new approach to growth.[8]

The critiques will continue, and in time it is possible that the idea of running an economy from a single number will be replaced. But this is unlikely to happen soon. An important reason for that is the ascent of China as a world power; a second reason is that change needs international agreement.

China's peoples are ready to reclaim their place as members of a respected world civilization—escaping the yoke of what they have long called their "century of humiliation" at the hands of the Western powers through wars and colonization. When judged by GDP, China is currently second only to the United States, and researchers are projecting that the country will take the top spot and become the world's richest economy inside the present decade.[9] China's statisticians are unlikely to agree a wholesale change of the rules before that happens.

The paradox here is that China's people and its policy makers have a depth of awareness of GDP's limitations that is not matched in the developed countries of the northern hemisphere, as I've seen during my visits to China to give talks and in meetings with government officials, academic researchers and think tanks. China's dash to industrial growth has had severe environmental consequences, which have been impossible to ignore, and the finger of blame has been pointed in the direction of GDP. In that time, GDP has also seeped into mainstream popular culture—Li Dakang is the growth-target-obsessed local Communist Party official in a popular TV soap, *In the Name of the People*.[10]

A decade ago, China's government even came close to implementing a 'Green GDP'—a version of the index that takes account of the environmental impacts of economic activity.[11] But the central government held back, partly because such an action would have put China out of step with global national accounting conventions, just as it was poised to become the world's GDP-topping country.

◆

The arguments for GDP to be replaced, or for it to stop being used, are powerful and compelling, but if that happened it would also mean losing GDP's strengths alongside its weaknesses—and GDP does have important strengths that need preserving. One of these is that it is set according to internationally agreed rules.

GDP's rules are set through the United Nations System of National Accounts (SNA). The rule-setters have not been oblivious to the critiques, or to developments in China. They can see that evidence is accumulating, and one of the biggest developments since this book's first edition is that they are preparing to take action. It's hard to overemphasize the importance of this.

Historically, the rules of GDP have been weighted in favour of the priorities of the richer countries, as economists Jacob Assa and Ingrid Kvangraven show in a paper just published.[12] The rules were set at a time when experts and policy makers from Europe and the United States were in a stronger position to set terms for the rest of the world. But GDP's rules are reviewed periodically and a process exists in which researchers from all UN member states have a voice to propose how GDP can change.

Discussions on the next revision to GDP have just started and are due to be finalized in 2025. Researchers and delegates from the developing countries are now much more involved than was previously the case. Moreover, for the first time, the rule-setters will consider how GDP could best take account of the environment.[13] Including the environment in GDP will compel governments to think twice before implementing environmentally harmful policies. And that will be no small achievement.

Of course, it isn't right that the world's economies are run like a car with one instrument, as Amartya Sen famously observed (see page xxviii). And it is far preferable for top policy makers to be able to recite more than one number. But change needs to be inclusive, and those advocating for change must find a way to ensure accountability for what comes next, ideally by working through a multilateral process. It cannot again be a case of expertise from the richer countries dominating over that from less developed ones. Expertise resides everywhere. As we've seen in the current pandemic, best practice in eliminating the virus has mostly been found in the countries of the southern hemisphere. The SNA process provides a route for all countries, rich and poor, to have an equal stake in deciding how the world's economies should measure what matters. Change, whether evolutionary or revolutionary, must be inclusive and accountable, too.

◆

I am grateful to Duncan Heath and colleagues at Icon Books for publishing this second edition, which also includes a new chapter on GDP and the Cold War (Chapter 5: "Red Star Over

Central Square"). I would also like to acknowledge Deborah Blum, Bettina Urcuioli and Victor McElheny of the Knight Science Journalism Program at the Massachusetts Institute of Technology in Cambridge; MIT's inspirational archivist Nora Murphy; and John Durant, Deborah Douglas and colleagues at the MIT Museum. I was a Knight Fellow during 2017/18, spending a memorable year researching this chapter and making a BBC Radio 4 documentary, *Surviving McCarthy*, on the scientists who found themselves caught in the net of McCarthyism.

This second edition is dedicated to the late, great David Corcoran, long-time science editor at *The New York Times*, who was my project adviser at MIT.

Readers are encouraged to get in touch using any of the following ways: I tweet from @EhsanMasood; I'm on LinkedIn at www.linkedin.com/in/ehsan-masood/; or if you prefer 20th-century email, you can find me at ehsanmasood@live.com.

PREFACE

This book tells the story of how a little-known formula emerged from the embers of the Great Depression and World War II to become the global standard for how to run an economy.

The story is told through the remarkable people who made it happen and those, equally remarkable, who foresaw trouble ahead. They were, in each case, the children of war and poverty, but they had a single-minded determination to create a better, more prosperous, more equitable, and more peaceful world than the one they had been born into. They had radically different ideas on how to go about it. And by and large, the ideas of only one group, those who wished to keep the status quo, prevailed.

My interest in the topic was sparked more than thirty years ago in a school economics class in Karachi where our teacher[1] introduced GDP by scribbling six symbols with white chalk on a slate blackboard. A few months later, in another economics class, this time in London, a different teacher scribbled the same symbols.

I remember wondering why the economy of one of the world's poorest countries, which at the time was also run by a military dictatorship, could be judged in the same way as one of the richest. I resolved to one day find out, and this book is the result of that quest.

Although this book draws on economics, history, politics, and science, it is not principally a work of history or of science; nor is it a textbook of macroeconomics. There are many and better accounts of what GDP is and how it is compiled.[2] There are also more comprehensive studies of economics and the environment—many referenced in the notes at the end of this book. *GDP* instead presents a narrative account, though one that is based mostly on authentic and sometimes neglected source materials, together with the results of hundreds of interviews. These have been conducted over nearly two decades during the course of my working life as a journalist navigating the boundary between science and policy.

GDP is an idea that began with good intentions but has undoubtedly outlived its usefulness. The answer, however, is not to abandon it, as some are advocating. More than anything, I want to show that GDP can change—and change so it can measure the things that matter. Indeed, it must if we are to begin to reverse many of the problems that have beset our societies, including rising inequality and possible environmental collapse.

What began as a useful measure to assess a country's prosperity and then measure it against its peers has trapped our societies and our leaders into a system from which we are unable to free ourselves. We must, and this book shows how we can.

Prologue

Lost History

*This is your heritage. Original documents are
now in your hands. If they are damaged or lost,
they cannot be replaced and a piece of history will
be lost.*

—Notice in the research room,
National Archives and Records
Administration, Washington, DC

t is late spring 2014 in Washington, DC, a couple of days
before the National Cherry Blossom Festival and I'm standing
on a windy Pennsylvania Avenue outside the offices of the US

National Archives. This giant of a building, a colossus of concrete and Corinthian columns, holds America's founding documents. Visitors from all over the world come here to catch a glimpse of the Declaration of Independence and the Gettysburg Address.

In the course of writing and researching this book, manuscript tourism has become something of a passion of mine, too. But I was here to look for a much less famous, indeed forgotten, piece of American history. I say "forgotten" because when I inquired from London some months earlier, the archivists weren't certain that they had the document I was looking for.

The paper in question is the first comprehensive listing of America's national income. It is called *National Income, 1929–32*; published at the end of January 1934, it was commissioned by a committee of the US Senate a year earlier. The task was handed to a talented young economist who had emigrated from Russia. For Simon Kuznets, *National Income* would be the job that would define the rest of his career. But it would also eventually estrange him from later US administrations. He would become an outsider to a process he helped create, in spite of later securing the Sveriges Riksbank Prize in Economic Sciences in Memory of Alfred Nobel, commonly known as the economics Nobel prize.

There are copies of Kuznets's document circulating online, but I wanted to view the original.

A solitary policeman greeted me at the front of the building. "Hello, I'm visiting from London, and I've come to view the first edition of the US national income," I explained, a little tentatively. He took a quick look at my bag and waved me through to the reception area, a cavernous space devoid of much natural light where I waited by a desk occupied by two of his colleagues.

I repeated my request, and after several phone calls to staff in different parts of the building, I was sent to a fourth officer. At this point I was beginning to wonder if they would let me through, when the police officer loudly said, "Belt." Nervously, I started to remove my belt. The officer broke into a smile and pointed to a small conveyor belt where I was to place my jacket and laptop. I had been cleared by security and was allowed to proceed.

With the security ritual over, I passed through a set of giant metal double doors, into an elevator that took me to the fifth-floor Research Room. There in a box file I hoped to find Kuznets's original document.

There was a six-page summary typed in the familiar Courier font of the time, double-spaced on paper only slightly yellow with age. The box also contained memos from the office of Senator Robert M. La Follette, who had commissioned the report, as well as letters from organizations asking the report's publishers for copies.

But the original document was missing. To this day no one knows where it has gone.

Introduction

The Great Invention

Washington, DC, December 7, 1999: members of President
Bill Clinton's economics team were assembled for a press
conference to announce the US government's achievement
of the century. The once invincible Federal Reserve Board chairman
Alan Greenspan was there, as was Clinton's top economics adviser,
Martin Baily; Commerce Secretary William Daley and Undersec-
retary Robert Shapiro were in the audience too. As the identity of
"one of the great inventions of the 20th century"[1] was revealed,
the only notable absentee was Clinton himself.

As US government agencies go, the relatively small Commerce Department is responsible for a collection of critical

government-run services, every one of which could have been a contender for the top prize. It is responsible for patents: the department issued 6 million of them in the 20th century (compared with 600,000 in the previous two centuries combined). It also developed the census and introduced the US National Weather Service. "We built the first atomic clock and we had a hand in creating the 911 emergency phone number," Daley said. "We are the smallest of the cabinet agencies, but we have accomplished the most—in my unbiased opinion," he added, injecting some humor into what could have been a very dry affair.[2]

But the Commerce Department's achievement of the century would be something else, something that one might ordinarily struggle to describe as an invention. The department's achievement of the century was a simple formula consisting of six letters: the formula for gross domestic product, or GDP.

"Think of it this way," Daley added. "A doctor can only make a diagnosis and prescribe a treatment after first sitting down and piecing together all the test results that have been taken. And economic policy makers are very much like doctors. So what the GDP accounts have done is to give us the tools to make those critical decisions." GDP, Shapiro would add, is "a living, growing monument to the ability of American economic genius."

◆

Governments from the earliest times have wanted to count and measure that which falls in their domain of influence. They have sought to map the distances between towns and cities; they have looked for ways of quantifying the nation's stock of natural resources, such as water and fossil fuels. Governments also like to know how much their citizens earn, so that they can levy the appropriate amount of tax.

But before Simon Kuznets's 1932 report on national income, governments in the Western Hemisphere had a weaker grip on this kind of knowledge. Unlike the more centrally planned states in the Soviet sphere of influence, countries such as America and Britain knew less about what their citizens earned, or the state of their economic production and consumption. At the same time, there was no agreed method to work out how much money was coming in and how much was being spent by the state. Countries didn't know with precision how much businesses were producing, nor did they have much of a sense of consumption patterns. This is what GDP was partly intended to fix. Forged in the fires of the Great Depression and the Second World War, the rationale behind GDP was that governments needed such data.

For arguably a majority of economists, and certainly for the assembled Washington gathering, GDP provided nations with an accurate account of their economies. The act of measurement also enabled, or coincided with, their nations becoming wealthier. The world's richest nations belong to a club called the Organization for Economic Cooperation and Development, or OECD. According to the OECD, today's nations are in effect ten times richer when their GDP of today is compared with their GDP in the early 1800s.[3] And it is no coincidence that this increase has coincided with the eighty years in which calculating a nation's GDP has been a global activity.

In his remarks to the gathering Daley flashed up a slide showing a simple chart with three vertical bars colored in black. The three bars represented America's GDP for three different years. Two of the three bars illustrated data for 1900 and 1929, before GDP was formally worked out. The third represented GDP in 1999.

America's GDP for 1900 was a lowly $290 billion. Twenty-nine years later it was $730 billion. In 1999, six decades after the great invention, US GDP had leapt to $9.2 trillion. Next to the other two years, that period appeared like a skyscraper on Daley's slide. "Gone are the bank runs, the financial panics, the deep and drawn out recessions, and the long lines of the unemployed," Daley said. "Obviously, the GDP accounts are not solely responsible for putting America's economy on a steadier track—as much as I'd like to make that claim. But no question about it: They have had a very positive effect on America's economic well-being."

The Washington party therefore had an extra-special resonance for the DC elite: at the same time as celebrating one of their own—William Daley—Alan Greenspan and colleagues were honoring a system of measurement that had contributed to the United States becoming the most powerful nation on Earth.

◆

The only hint of caution that morning came, ironically enough, from Greenspan. This was still some years before the crash of 2008, and the Federal Reserve Board chairman was at the height of his powers and regarded as the chief architect and steward of America's seemingly unending run of prosperity. "I cannot say what the size of the economy will be 1 year from today or 100 years from now," Daley joked. "But I can say that when we reach the next milestone—$10 trillion—will depend a lot on . . . Chairman Greenspan."

Amid the celebrations, however, the Federal Reserve Board chairman had a warning for his audience. In the very mildest of terms, he said that it would be wrong to conflate GDP with quality of life, and he cautioned that an increase in one did not necessarily mean an increase in the other. Just because a country such as the United States has high rates of economic growth, it doesn't automatically mean it will enjoy a high quality of life, Greenspan said. To illustrate what he meant, Greenspan asked his audience to compare how people in the northern states cooled themselves during the summer months compared with folks in the South. While the northern residents were fortunate to enjoy cool sea breezes, those down south had to turn up the air-conditioning. While both, you could say, enjoyed an equally high quality of life, in GDP terms, the air-conditioned group would come out on top. "The wonderful breezes you get up in northern Vermont during the summer, which eliminates the requirement for air conditioning, doesn't show up in the GDP," Greenspan added.[4]

Greenspan was correct. GDP is neither a measure of welfare nor an indicator of well-being. That is because it is not set up to recognize important aspects of our lives that are not captured by the acts of spending and investing. There is no room in GDP for volunteering or housework, for example; nor does it recognize that there is value in community or in time spent with families. More measurable things such as damage to our environment are also left out, as is job satisfaction. GDP doesn't even measure the state of jobs.

Greenspan's was by no means a lone voice cautioning against reading too much into GDP beyond what it says about the state of production, or spending, or incomes. From the earliest days, its inventors, including Simon Kuznets and the British economist

John Maynard Keynes, understood that it is not really a measure of prosperity, and Kuznets in particular became skeptical of the way in which his invention was being used as a proxy for this. As far back as 1922, the English banker and statistician Josiah Stamp questioned why national income did not include the value of housework or volunteering and remarked that the trend seemed to be to value those things that are important to rich people.[5]

Today, such voices have been joined by many more, including the leaders of developed and developing nations. Together with government ministers and civil servants, academics, campaigners, and business folk, they recognize that GDP has strengths but also flaws, and they want change. But they cannot agree on what could or should change, and they are even less certain about how change could happen.

Many support the idea that world leaders should be encouraged to follow a "dashboard" of numbers, of which GDP could be one, alongside indicators of the state of a nation's health, education, employment, living standards, environment, and well-being. This dashboard might include the Human Development Index, a pioneering idea that in a single number captures life expectancy, literacy and schooling alongside income. The HDI was created more than twenty-five years ago as an alternative to GDP but would stand for better things, according to one of its architects, the Pakistani economist Mahbub ul Haq.[6] A dashboard of alternatives to GDP might also include Gross National Happiness, an innovation from the landlocked state of Bhutan. India's Nobel Prize-winning economist Amartya Sen famously said that if you wouldn't drive a car by looking at a single indicator, say, the fuel or temperature gauge, why adopt such a flawed principle to managing an entire economy?

Sen has a point, and I for one wish that such a multifaceted approach became the norm. But the practice of the past eight decades tells us that our leaders are not quite ready to embrace the complexity that Sen and so many others are advocating. If anything, in our era of Big Data, the volume and frequency of information are greater than at any time in history. Policy makers, at the same time, are on the whole less expert than they once were. More than ever they need an index that can capture complex phenomena and represent them in easy-to-digest formats. That is quite possibly why, in the years since the introduction of the HDI and the many indicators that have come in its wake, one index continues to reign, and that is GDP. While it is true that nations are now better informed on the alternatives, it is GDP on which our leaders are judged. Even if every single one of the alternatives on the dashboard were to show a positive sign, it is economic growth (for which read GDP) that matters at the ballot box for any serving head of government and his or her finance team. So long as growth remains the overriding objective, that effectively means there will always be a higher priority for economic policies that result in higher production and higher consumption, no matter what the costs of those policies may be.

If we are to assume that GDP isn't going away anytime soon, then the challenge is not about introducing a better alternative indicator, because that won't make a difference to economic policy making. The challenge has to be to change GDP itself so that it is better able to represent the things that matter to us.

One

GDP and Its Discontents

*The government are very keen on amassing
statistics. They collect them, add them, raise them
to the nth power, take the cube root and prepare
wonderful diagrams. But you must never forget that
every one of these figures comes in the first instance
from the chowky dar (village watchman in India),
who just puts down what he damn pleases.*

> —Josiah Stamp, *Some Economic
> Factors in Modern Life* (1929)

GDP is the world's principal measure of economic growth. It is regarded by many as a proxy for prosperity, a single number meant to indicate if countries and their citizens are doing well or badly.

1

In practical terms (and for the purposes of this book) GDP is defined as an indicator of spending.[1] It is the sum of what we spend every day, from the contents of our weekly shopping to large capital spending by businesses. GDP also includes many of the myriad things that our governments pay to produce,[2] from relatively inexpensive things such as libraries and streetlamps to naval dockyards and nuclear weapons, whose cost is calculated in the billions.

In most countries GDP is published every quarter, following surveys of households, businesses, and government spending carried out by an arm of the government known as an office for national statistics. These surveys take place on an epic scale. In 2014, the UK's Office for National Statistics sent out more than 1.5 million survey forms and sampled almost 350,000 businesses. Businesses especially do not have any choice. Under the Statistics for Trade Act 1947 it is compulsory for a business to take part in GDP data collection if asked to do so.[3]

The Internet heaves with global GDP rankings. If you measure GDP per person, then the countries with the highest GDP tend to be from the Nordic region. If you measure GDP in absolute terms, then the top-ranked nation is the United States. By the end of 2015, America's GDP was about $18 trillion. China's was $11 trillion, in second place, though fast catching up. Britain's was a more modest $4.3 trillion.

Like all league tables, global rankings of GDP are watched hawkishly by those whose futures depend on their position in the table, and that includes presidents and prime ministers, ministers of finance especially, and opposition political parties too. And, as with any kind of ranking—like those of football teams or universities—those being watched make it their business to do what they can to maintain their position and, if possible, to best it.

GDP is also monitored closely by an assortment of outside individuals and organizations, including central banks, whose job it is to manage the nation's money, as well as financial commentators, and those who make money by predicting what the next quarter's GDP figures will be. Then there are international institutions such as the OECD, the financial markets, and of course the media in all its varied forms. Last but not least, GDP is a huge topic in economics education, from schools to university seminar rooms.

GDP in Symbols

I first learned about GDP in a high school economics class in the early 1980s. One afternoon our teacher picked up a piece of white chalk and wrote the following six symbols on a blackboard:

$$Y = C + I + G + (X - M)$$

C, he told us, is what consumers spend in the shops.
I is what businesses spend.
G is spending by governments.
X is what companies sell to customers abroad.
M is what we buy from sellers overseas.

Put them all together and you get the total of a country's GDP (Y).

Recently in my parents' garage I rediscovered my economics lecture notes, still held together in a red ring binder.[4] Among the papers was a copy of an examination paper that included a question on GDP. Candidates were asked to define economic growth and then "give one disadvantage" of economic growth. Intriguingly, we were never taught that growth was automatically a good thing. On the contrary, as students we were encouraged to understand and debate the pros and cons and then make up our own minds.

The quarterly announcement of GDP figures ranks as one of the great rituals of modern political life. It is a day infused with drama and theater, both real and manufactured. News of the announcement of GDP figures will be trailed by the media beforehand. If GDP is more than in the previous three months, senior politicians of the party in government will take to the air, crowing about their prowess in economic management. But if GDP drops, even temporarily, or if it flatlines, opposition voices will call for heads to roll.

Even the smallest of falls is seized on by political opponents as evidence of economic incompetence, as George Osborne, the then-chancellor of the exchequer, learned in 2012. Britain's GDP figures between April and June 2012 (published at the end of July in that same year) showed that GDP had contracted by 0.7 percent.[5] This was no sudden drop, and the figures later recovered, but it was the steepest quarterly fall since 2009 and there was a discernible sense of panic in the country. Many (including a few in the government's coalition partners from the centrist Liberal Democrat party) seized the opportunity to call for Osborne to resign. Newspaper headline writers were even less kind, with the left-leaning *Independent* dubbing Osborne, who had been in the role just one year, Britain's "work-experience chancellor."[6] Osborne and his prime minister, David Cameron, never made the same mistake again. All leaders of all nations know that their electoral success depends in large part on helping their citizens prosper, which means that GDP figures can only point in one direction.

Paradoxically, just as Britain's GDP took a momentary dive, other economic indicators were heading upward. For example, in the same three months, from April to June 2012, an extra 200,000 people were in jobs compared with the previous quarter and most of these were working in the private sector. Between June and August unemployment fell again by a further 50,000.[7] Inflation meanwhile remained historically low, at around 2.4 percent, and more people were taking loans to purchase houses compared with the same period in the previous year.[8] Even receipts from value-added tax (an indirect tax on spending) were up by 6 percent, suggesting that consumers were confident enough to spend in the shops.

So, while on the one hand GDP was falling, several other economic indicators were more positive, suggesting that the indicator for falling economic growth was not on its own a sign that everything is going to pot.

The opposite can also be the case, however. Rising GDP does not automatically mean that all is well with a country's people and their finances.

Take debt, for example. Countries with healthy GDP figures can include large numbers of people in debt. That is in part because all those loans, unpaid credit card bills, and mortgages show that people are spending money somewhere, and higher consumer spending is a positive indicator for GDP. When, in 2013, the UK growth figures began heading back upward, one of the reasons for the turnaround was the introduction of a generous government-funded home-buying scheme called "Help to Buy." Between April 2013 and December 2014 the scheme helped unlock the sale of houses worth more than $13 billion. In helping their economy to grow, British householders were taking on another $10 billion in debt.[9]

As in the UK, the average US household, too, owes much more than it earns in a year. Between 2000 and 2011, median household debt increased from $50,000 to $70,000.[10] And yet, as former commerce secretary William Daley reminded his audience celebrating the department's greatest achievement, this was also the nation's longest period of continuous, uninterrupted economic growth.

In the UK, the Labour government of Tony Blair would similarly trumpet the longest period of uninterrupted growth in modern times.[11] The growth figures on their own, however, told us nothing about people in debt; nor did they record the numbers of people receiving free-food handouts from food-aid charities, or from food banks. The numbers of individuals in the UK given emergency food supplies have been climbing steadily. In 2005 there were around 2,800. That increased to 25,000 in 2008–2009. At time of writing, just over a million people needed a three-day supply of food in 2014–2015.[12] That is in the world's sixth-richest economy. One reason, I would argue, why our leading policy makers failed to spot this is because in part they were looking at just one number, and that was economic growth, as measured by GDP.

❖

As we saw from the crash of 2008, GDP can mask poverty or social unrest, because it is unable to record people in debt but also because it does not measure those who don't have jobs. For an even more powerful example of a country where healthy GDP figures concealed deep-seated social and economic problems, we need to consider the case of Tunisia.

Tunisia is now famous as the crucible for the uprisings in 2011, commonly referred to as the Arab revolutions, and frequently mischaracterized as the Arab Spring. The revolutions were ignited when Mohamed Bouazizi, a young street vendor, set himself alight on December 17, 2010, in the middle of busy traffic in his hometown of Sidi Bouzid. The young man, his family's sole breadwinner, took this extreme action because he did not have enough money to bribe his city's corrupt police; such a bribe would allow him to continue trading. After a fruitless altercation with a state official, he doused himself with gasoline and set himself alight, shouting, "How do you expect me to make a living?" Mohamed Bouazizi died from his burns eighteen days later.

Until the day of Bouazizi's suicide, Tunisia, according to economists and watchers of world politics, including yours truly, was a prosperous and relatively modern liberal Arab state with a growing economy. To be sure, it was no democracy and had been ruled for the previous twenty-three years by the dictator Zine El Abidine Ben Ali. It didn't really matter that Ben Ali ran a hated police state. We all loved him because he was an economic liberal who opened up Tunisian markets to international trade, especially from the European Union. Ben Ali's policies were enriching a small Tunisian middle class, which consequently had the finances to shop for more expensive things. That led to an increase in consumer spending. At the same time, businesses were investing and income from exports was going up, especially in clothing, crude oil, and high technology. In 2010 Tunisia's GDP stood at around $4,169 per person, considerably higher than the $3,211 it had been in 2005.[13] For this Ben Ali was praised by international bodies, including the European Union and the OECD.

What we couldn't see is that around one person in eight of working age in Tunisia had no job. Among men under the age of twenty-five that figure was as high as one in three, according to some estimates. But because unemployment isn't recorded in the GDP figures, the country looked to be the model growing economy. The received wisdom was that as long as the GDP figures kept increasing, the country was on the right track. Rising spending was supposed to mean that Tunisians were getting richer, and so it didn't really matter if there weren't that many jobs now, as they would inevitably come with the country's greater wealth.

Of course we now know that nothing of the sort happened. Tunisia's rate of job creation never kept up with its rising GDP. Its wealth was being concentrated among a small number of people.

This points to another flaw in GDP: it provides no way of demonstrating whether there is rising inequality in a society. Even in America, while GDP has been steadily rising, median household income has not been keeping up. According to data from the US Census Bureau, incomes and GDP were more or less on the same upward curve until 1999, almost a decade before the financial crisis of 2008. And then they diverged. While GDP continued on broadly the same path, household incomes for America's middle classes stopped growing somewhat abruptly, started to fall and continued to do so until 2004, began to rise again, and then dropped sharply in 2008. In 2013, median household incomes in America were at the same level as they were in the mid to late 1990s.[14]

The conclusion is that, since 1999, growth in the American economy has not translated into prosperity for the nation's middle classes. Fifteen percent of Americans, or some 45 million people, are living below the poverty line. The *New York Times* summed up the Census Bureau's finding with the headline in its September 16, 2014, edition: "You Can't Feed a Family with G.D.P."

◆

GDP hides other problems too. In spite of repeated criticism and from much earlier times, it has consistently failed to value volunteering. Nor does it value housework, job satisfaction, time with friends and family, or other means through which we experience quality of life.

GDP also fails to include any measure of the economic impact of environmental degradation. For example, countries that are poor in an economic sense but rich in other ways, such as an abundance of plant and animal species, known as biodiversity, will rank low in the GDP tables. At the same time, GDP has the ability to reward countries that destroy environmental resources. For example, if forest land is cleared to grow crops or build houses or factories, then that will result in an increase in GDP, because the acts of building, producing, and farming mean more production, more consumption; more spending. If, for example, more pedestrians are hospitalized because of the effects of inhaling vehicular fumes, then there is more public health spending, and more public health spending helps to increase GDP.

What this means is that GDP could well be acting as an obstacle to tackling some of the pressing environmental needs of our time, such as slowing down climate change or reducing the rate of species loss. While there are more than 100 different international conventions and treaties that promise to protect the environment, we know that climate change is heading into dangerous territory and the rate of species loss is now higher than at any time since the last mass extinction.[15] Undoubtedly one reason for this is the desire to maximize growth, as measured by GDP.

For the past two decades, my work as a journalist straddling the boundary between research and policy making has involved

9

conversations with politicians, civil servants, and their advisers on most of the world's major continents. Increasingly, these conversations have centered on what is becoming known as a global "race." Nations are desperate to become the most innovative economy by investing more in their science, technology, industries, and so on, with progress measured by GDP. Even those ministers with responsibility for protecting the environment recognize that their efforts will always be constrained by the fact that more senior colleagues (heads of government and ministers of finance) are fixated on growth above all else.

Even as the big international agencies, such as those in the United Nations and the World Bank, continually claim to be working toward a world where people live safer, cleaner, and more fulfilled lives, the central thrust of their policy recommendations is growth. And the main measure of growth, as we have seen, is unable to capture well-being or the environment.

If it is true that GDP remains the only number that influential politicians, the markets, the banks, the media, and the commentators pay attention to, then the solution cannot be more alternative indicators; nor can it be a dashboard. The solution has to be to value the things that matter and then incorporate this value into the GDP accounts.

There will be more on this in later chapters, but let's begin with the recent history of GDP and how we got to where we are.

Two

The Fight for the Formula

It is not easy for a free community to organise for war. We are not accustomed to listen to experts or prophets. Our strength lies in an ability to improvise. Yet an open mind to untried ideas is also necessary.

—John Maynard Keynes,
How to Pay for the War (1940)

The crash of 2008 and the recession that followed it are often talked of as a second Great Depression. But there's no comparing our most recent banking crisis with the misery that incinerated lives in the 1930s. Life for many today is difficult, certainly. But the Great Depression was a disaster.

In America at the height of the economic slump between 1932 and 1933, somewhere between one in three and one in four men of working age was out of work. One million families lost their farms and two million people became homeless. Families in jobless, homeless, and indebted circumstances were becoming ill, and disease was leading to death on a horrific scale.

At the same time, after the stock market crash of 1929, banks had either locked their doors or were in the process of slamming them shut to protect their remaining deposits from panic-stricken customers intent on emptying their bank accounts.

The Depression was deep, and in the United States both the federal government and Congress were in disarray over what to do about it. Part of the problem in knowing what to do was an almost complete lack of data on the health of the economy. This is sometimes difficult to appreciate in our age of Big Data, but before GDP the volume of data available to the public was a fraction of what it is today.

The only similarity is that both then and now, governments were desperate to know how economies could be kick-started, and especially how new jobs could be created. But to create new jobs, governments needed to first know how many were employed. To raise living standards, they needed to know what people were earning.

Among the lawmakers most concerned about the absence of meaningful information on the numbers of people in jobs or the value of factory goods was the Republican senator for Wisconsin, Robert La Follette Jr.

La Follette was a centrist Republican in that he championed relief for the unemployed and also supported government spending to create jobs. He was also keen that the federal government should begin compiling statistics and in 1931 presided over the following piece of political theater to prove his point.

At the time, members of the Senate were holding an inquiry into the state of American manufacturing. Congressional inquiries are an opportunity for elected representatives to ask searching questions of those government employees who are paid to carry out Congress's wishes, but who rarely appear in public. Witnesses are called to testify in what can be a tense and sometimes gladiatorial atmosphere. In 1931 the sacrificial lamb was Frederick Dewhurst, an official in the Department of Commerce who was ordered to give evidence before the US Senate. Judging by the transcript of the exchange,[1] Dewhurst probably didn't know what was about to hit him.

It is worth reproducing something of that exchange:

> CHAIRMAN (LA FOLLETTE): *I would like to direct your attention to the available labor statistics. What would you say about the statistics of unemployment? Have we any?*
>
> DEWHURST: *Not any, except for one month in the history of the republic. That was April 1930. The census taken in that month gives a sort of benchmark.*
>
> C: *And they took a sample test later on in January?*
>
> D: *A sample in January 1931, of 19 cities only.*
>
> C: *But aside from that, we have nothing?*
>
> D: *No, we have no direct measure; we can infer or estimate or guess on the basis of changes in employment.*
>
> C: *You can go around Robin Hood's barn to get it, but so far as actual statistics are concerned, we have not any; is that correct?*

D: *Yes.*

C: *What about payroll statistics? We are woefully lacking in wage statistics, are we not?*

D: *Yes.*

C: *Now let us consider statistics on consumer purchases.*

D: *In the first place, we do not have a very good coverage of the total field of consumer purchases. In the second place we have lost the identity of commodities completely by the time they get to the consumer, except for a few, such as automobiles.*

C: *You cannot answer the question.*

D: *I would hate to guess it within 100 percent.*

C: *What about statistics on savings and investments?*

D: *. . . We do not know much about that except from the published statistics of new security issues.*

C: *How about investment credit? Do you make the same answer?*

D: *That is the same answer; yes; except that it is more so.*

At this point in the proceedings the transcript shows Democratic Senator Morris Sheppard, one of the founders of the temperance movement, stepping in to protect Dewhurst from further self-harm. Sheppard asks the civil servant whether he thinks that a more complete picture of the US economy would "be of benefit to the government and to the people of the country." Dewhurst's reply is telling.

"In my opinion, it would be most desirable," he says, before adding this coded warning: "May I add that a statistician is prejudiced in that he always wants more statistics. Statisticians are never satisfied."

La Follette's plan was to persuade the US government to find out and then publish what people were earning and to establish whether earnings had been increasing or decreasing in the years leading up to 1932. In June of that year he got what he wanted; the Senate passed a resolution ordering the commerce secretary to carry out an estimate of total US national income for 1929, 1930, and 1931 and to provide this information before December 15, 1933.

That task was assigned to Simon Kuznets (1901–1985), who had emigrated to America from Russia at age twenty-two, in 1922, five years after the Russian Revolution. Kuznets started work on producing national income accounts the following month, January 1933, and submitted his final report to the Senate a year later, on January 4, 1934.[2]

When the Senate asked for an estimate of the value of the US national income, there was no precedent, nor a template for how this should be done. It meant that Kuznets had to invent the method for calculating total national income for an economy the size of the United States. He had to do so in less than a year with a small team and with none of the infrastructure for collecting data that we take for granted today—not a single computer; not even a hand-held electronic calculator.

Kuznets began work by compiling lists of America's different industrial sectors, such as agriculture, mining, and factories, from where data would need to be found. He was given a small team of three "senior assistants" and five "statistical clerks." Together they hit the road, visiting factories, mines, and farms, interviewing owners and managers, and writing down figures in notebooks. Once a notebook was filled, it would be sent to the Department of Commerce in Washington to be checked or revised. Books would often be sent back and forth between Kuznets's team, Washington, and the original source, until anomalies and queries were ironed out.

True to his word, Kuznets delivered on time and the Senate published his work as a 261-page report entitled *National Income, 1929–32*.[3] The report's price tag was the princely sum of 20 US cents and it turned out to be a surprise best-seller, with its 4,500-copy print run selling out well within the year.[4]

Kuznets and his team made no effort to varnish their findings and confirmed what was plain to anyone at that time. Between 1929 and 1932, US national income had almost halved. The total income distributed to individuals in 1929 had been $81 billion. In 1930 it dropped to $75.4 billion. The following year it was $63.3 billion, and in 1932 it had crashed to $49 billion, confirming the misery and devastation everyone could see around them.

Moreover, no sector had been immune to the crisis. Agriculture income had dropped from $6.3 billion in 1929 to $3.4 billion in 1932. During the same period, income from construction had collapsed from $3.1 billion to $0.9 billion. The biggest fall had been in manufacturing, from $18.1 billion in 1929 to $8.4 billion three years later.

Salaried staff on the whole suffered comparatively less (their incomes fell from $5.7 billion to $3.4 billion). In contrast, incomes of those on (less secure) daily and weekly wages crashed from $17.2 billion in 1929 to $6.8 billion in 1932.

There was, however, one sector of the economy where incomes not only had stayed constant but had even managed to register a small increase. This was the column marked "Government." According to Simon Kuznets and his team, between 1929 and 1932 income distributed by government entities was up from $6.5 billion to $6.8 billion, reflecting a small increase in public works programs.[5]

In many ways, the rise in government spending isn't as intriguing as is its inclusion in Kuznets's national accounts. This is because, for much of his professional life, Simon Kuznets fought the inclusion of government spending in GDP. Data from businesses formed the cornerstone of his methodology, and he was confident in the quality of the data he and his team had gathered. Government data was something else. Kuznets believed quite stubbornly that government spending does not belong in the national accounts in part because spending by the state doesn't make for a very productive economy. When governments spend money, they're not producing anything new, just recycling what is there. At the same time, he took the view, as do many economists today, that spending by governments crowds out spending by businesses. If governments produce a good or a service, then that is a good or service denied to business, which, ultimately, isn't good for economies. Such an approach, as we shall see, would put him on a collision course with his US government colleagues in the years ahead.

◆

Although for the next decade Kuznets would be Washington's go-to man for all things national accounting, a new generation of economists working for the US government had become uneasy about Kuznets's accounts as being the sum total of private incomes.

By the late 1930s the drums of war were getting louder and leaders in Europe and America felt that conflict with Germany was a matter of when, not if. Many had either fought in or lived through the First World War, and they knew that they needed to be better prepared militarily a second time around. That meant having deeper knowledge of what the government had available to spend to go to war. Handguns, rifles, tanks, battleships, and fighter aircraft would all cost, as would professional soldiers and volunteer conscripts. Businesses, too, would be affected. Factories would need to be commandeered for the war effort, and that would mean making and selling fewer of their normal products.

Herein lay the federal government's big problem. According to Kuznets's methodology for economic measurement, not only was there no space for the state's finances, but its absence would make a wartime economy look even smaller. That is because people would be earning less; because business would be producing less and because the vastness of government spending would be kept off the books. US government economists needed a system of measurement that would go beyond adding up private incomes, as Kuznets had done, and include the role of government.

The problem for this younger generation of economists was that Kuznets was having none of this. The future Nobel laureate resisted his colleagues' attempts to change his methods and include government spending in the national accounts, so much so that they looked for an alternative champion.

Such a champion would emerge in the shape of intellectual-cum-socialite John Maynard Keynes (1883–1946).[6]

◆

John Maynard Keynes (known to his friends as Maynard) was certainly a one-off. To many he was the 20th century's greatest economist, though certainly not an economist in the conventional sense. He was a part of the generation who lived through the end of empire, the Boer War, the Great Depression, and two world wars. He was a polymath, gifted with unusual powers of curiosity and a remarkable ability to influence.

Keynes had that rare gift of being able to persuade. Using a combination of confidence, intellect, charm, dogged persistence, and a certain amount of bullying, he believed he could persuade not just his fellow economists, but also those in disciplines outside economics, and those with no connection to academia at all, to come round to his point of view. Keynes was also a compulsive writer of newspaper articles, an assiduous builder of networks of friends in high places, and an extraordinarily successful investor. His efforts would not always succeed, and many of those he encountered, especially in the United States, found him insufferably pompous. But there is no doubting he knew how to work the corridors of politics, which he would do through sheer force of argument and his not inconsiderable presence. These are among the reasons why the British economic historian Lord Robert Skidelsky, author of a three-volume biography of Keynes, calls him "The Master."[7]

Keynes wasn't born lowly, but neither was he superrich. He came from a family of empire-era scholars that included Charles Darwin before him. These were men born into relative privilege, and they benefited directly from being part of the British imperial experience. But rather than profit from that experience as so many did, they instead chose a path of scholarship and discovery.

So how did Keynes put the *G* in the GDP equation?

Let's begin with the book that put Keynes on the world economic and political map. While Darwin is famous for *On the Origin of Species*, Keynes's magnum opus is called *The General Theory of Employment, Interest and Money*. It was a publishing sensation when it appeared in 1936. It is still in print, still much more readable than your average economics text, and, perhaps because of this, still consulted by world leaders in times of economic crisis. It is the primary source for any argument in favor of increasing public spending.

At the time of the Depression, Keynes was also consumed with the question of how to get more people back into jobs and how to help businesses become more productive. Keynes's prescription was radical for the times, and he called it "demand." What he meant by "demand" is that if private businesses were unable to create jobs during a severe depression, then governments needed to step in and spend money on big projects, such as roads, bridges, buildings, even towns. These projects in turn would create the kinds of jobs that would last for some time, which would help people get back to work and acquire new skills. Such an idea has become known as a Keynesian stimulus. It was also the framework for President Roosevelt's New Deal and was applied again to deal with the latest banking and financial crisis. After 2008, across Europe and America, governments poured billions into expensive schemes such as roads, dams, and bridges (or "shovel-ready" projects, in the words of President Barack Obama), to help people get back into employment.[8]

But the idea of a Keynesian stimulus was—and continues to be—opposed, especially on the center-right of politics. That is because, as Kuznets pointed out, governments on their own are not productive in any economic sense. They merely spend what they receive, and that is largely from the taxes they collect from their citizens. Large government expenditure according to this view risks spending beyond what a country can afford. Also, during Keynes's time, the other great exemplar of massive government spending to boost an economy happened to be one Adolf Hitler, not a model to be imitated.[9]

According to the alternative view, the most important factor in creating jobs is what is called "supply." "Supply" in this context means that if businesses are left to get on with making and selling things, then jobs will follow. Instead of thinking they can help, governments need to do the opposite: they ought to get out of the way and let businesses supply goods and services. That will create demand; it will create jobs and consumer spending, all of which will keep the economy going. On no account, according to a more extreme interpretation of this view, must government provide money for jobs, impose barriers on business, or write new rules or enact new regulations. Recessions and depressions happen when governments try to meddle. Even if they think they're meddling for the right reasons, the results will invariably be catastrophic, which is why the role of government is simply to stand aside, almost not to exist.

The idea that supply creates its own demand is often attributed to an eighteenth-century French businessman and economist named Jean-Baptiste Say. In fact economists misleadingly call it Say's Law. I say "misleadingly" because it's not really a law as this word is understood in the scientific world. Science, too, is just as argumentative as economics. But an idea in science gets to be elevated to legal status only if it can be proved, or verified beyond doubt—essentially when the arguments largely stop. If you kick a football, for example, few will debate its trajectory. It will behave in a way predicted by theory and confirmed through experiment, according to one of Newton's laws of motion. In contrast, when an economist uses the word "law," he or she usually means a theory or a hypothesis. It is an idea, yet to be confirmed, and subject to differing opinions. That is very much the case with Say's Law.

A modern example of the use of Say's Law could be the rise of technology giants such as Google and Apple. Both these companies have created massively successful products. Because these products did not exist previously, you could say that their supply created demand, which, in turn, has created millions of new jobs around the world. Supporters of Say's Law claim that these are all jobs in which government has had little or no role. But critics of Say's Law, such as the economist Mariana Mazzucato, would argue the opposite. They say that much employment creation involves some role for government. The tech giants, for example, wouldn't have a business were it not for the Internet and the World Wide Web. The Internet was created by scientists funded by the US government; the web was funded almost in its entirety by the governments of Europe through the European Organization for Nuclear Research, CERN, in Geneva.[10]

Until the Great Depression, Keynes did not fundamentally disagree with Say's Law, but once employment levels began to fall off a cliff, he began to do something that many scientists find quite difficult: in the face of a changing situation, he started to think differently and to ask questions. Was unemployment rising because businesses were producing things that no one wanted to buy? he asked. Or was it more likely that jobs were being lost because people had become too poor to spend any money in the shops? Was it this lack of demand that meant entire industries were becoming idle, laying off workers in the thousands?

At some point during this period Keynes concluded that he had to change his mind regarding Say's Law. The problem of unemployment during a depression, he now believed, was not one of supply but one of a lack of *effective* demand. This is where consumers are in a position to pay for something. It is not demand in the abstract. According to Keynes, one way to stimulate such demand was for governments to spend money and create jobs. Keynes convinced himself and others that the urge to consume pushed economic activity forward and the urge not to consume held economic activity back. In one lecture in 1933 he described his ideas on demand and consumption using an imaginary scientific experiment on chickens.

Imagine, he asked his audience, that scientists could remove that part of a hen's brain that controls the urge to eat. This hen is completely normal, except that if you put a pile of wheat in front of it, the hen won't touch it. The hen is so uninterested in eating that it eventually starves to death. Something similar, Keynes concluded, was happening to the world's economies after the Great Depression. There was no shortage of supply, he said, because businesses had the ability to produce whatever society demanded, whether wheat or chaff. What was killing consumers was that they were unable to consume the existing wheat. The wheat was there. They just couldn't eat it. It's similar to the kind of argument used sometimes to explain famine. Hunger doesn't happen because of a lack of food, but because what food there is doesn't reach the people who need it the most.

◈

In Chapter 18 of *The General Theory*, Keynes set out in more detail his arguments for public spending in a depression. He argued that businesses cannot just be left to get on with things because, in a depression, there will be few with the means to purchase. In making his arguments he divided expenditure into two components: spending by households, which he called consumption, and spending by businesses, which he called investment.[11]

According to Keynes, if consumption increased, if more people *were able to* buy goods and services, then businesses would spend more. When businesses spent more on goods and services as well as on premises and machinery, then that would lead to an increase in investment. Taken together, an increase in consumption and an increase in investment would cause the national income to increase.

Keynes according to his biographer deliberately chose not to write his idea in mathematical form, but if we did it could be summarized as:

Economic Output = Consumption (C) + Investment (I)

But we need to bear two things in mind: First, Keynes had not yet written his ideas as a table or a formula. And second, although his book provides a rationale for greater government spending, he hadn't at this point included public spending in his definition of how to measure an economy. That would come next.[12]

◆

In 1939, when Adolf Hitler invaded Poland, Britain declared war on Germany, and Keynes's thoughts turned to the same question of war financing that the younger US economists had been asking before him.

"It is not easy for a free community to organise for war. We are not accustomed to listen to experts or prophets," he mused in a series of articles for the London *Times*. "Our strength lies in an ability to improvise. Yet an open mind to untried ideas is also necessary," he would say.[13] One such "untried idea" was figuring out the income and outgoings of the British government. As it was for his US counterparts, this was the basic knowledge on which all other thinking around wartime finance needed to be built, and Keynes, like Senator Robert La Follette Jr., was incredulous that this information was not easy to find. "The statistics from which to build up these estimates are very inadequate," he would say. "Every government since the last war has been unscientific and obscurantist, and has regarded the collection of essential facts as a waste of money."

In the absence of official estimates, Keynes drew heavily on the work of one of his Cambridge colleagues, the statistician Colin Clark (1905–1989). Clark was an obsessive collector of data on the national income. He was the nearest that Britain had to a Simon Kuznets, although he was a Kuznets with no official mandate.[14] "There is no one to-day who does not mainly depend on the brilliant *private* efforts of Mr Colin Clark," Keynes would write. "But in the absence of statistics that only a government can collect, he could often do no better than make a brave guess."[15]

Colin Clark, just like Kuznets, was mainly interested in collecting data on private incomes. And as with Kuznets there was no role for government in his national income scheme. For Keynes there was no point in studying wartime finance if government spending data couldn't be found. In the very least he needed such data to work out how much the state could expect in taxation and so arranged for Clark's tables to be updated.

Keynes calculated the size of the UK economy as of March 31, 1939, to be £4.85 billion. He subdivided this total under three headings:

"The consumption of the public": £3.71 billion
"Privately-owned capital equipment": £290 million
"Cost of the services provided by government": £850 million

He converted his *Times* articles into a book, and at eighty-eight pages long, *How to Pay for the War* is one of Keynes's shortest books. Its main function was to help the government and the public understand the nature of British wartime finances. But there, buried in a table on page 14, was the final variable in our GDP formula—the *G*, for government spending, which he calculated to be £850 million. In 1940, six years after Simon Kuznets had presented his national income estimates to the Senate, Keynes had written down in a table the basis for what today is the formula for GDP.

$$GDP = C + I + G$$

Keynes's London *Times* articles and his book *How to Pay for the War* caught the attention of policy makers. In Britain, it prompted the Treasury to take a closer look at government finances and to have them published for the first time the following year, in 1941. But in America, it arguably had a more powerful effect. Keynes's book supported those economists who were moving away from Kuznets's insistence that an economy be measured as the sum of private incomes, and who wanted to find a way to include government spending in the national accounts. They were in the Department of Commerce, as we have seen, but another group was working in the Office of Price Administration and Civilian Supply (OPACS). This was the government agency responsible for mobilizing resources for the war, and they, as much as the Commerce Department, needed a handle on the nation's finances. But such was Simon Kuznets's hold on accounting methodology that these younger officials were finding it hard to have an impact.

By 1940 and with America's role in World War II looming, OPACS desperately needed to know what government spending would look like. They tried to argue that including government spending would likely boost the size of an economy. However, others countered by saying that doing so could also result in a post-war economy shrinking once government spending on armaments, for example, was cut back.

We know that Keynes had a former student at OPACS, and during his 1941 visit to America to negotiate the lend-lease agreements, they met at Keynes's suite at the Mayflower Hotel and exchanged documents.[16] One of those documents was an estimate of US gross national product, which is worked out in a similar way to GDP.[17] This exercise gave them an idea about how much America would have to spend on the war.

The problem that OPACS faced was Kuznets, who protested against the new system. This quite possibly prompted Keynes to note, "There is too wide a gap here in Washington between the intellectual outlook of the older people and that of the younger. But I have been greatly struck during my visit by the quality of the younger economists and civil servants in the Administration."[18]

But by this time, the momentum was turning against Kuznets as Keynes's international influence grew. Kuznets began to be criticized in the pages of influential journals, which helped Keynesian economists in the US administration to join the debate and to say that they, too, agreed that Kuznets was wrong to ignore spending by the state, and that the US national accounts had to change to reflect this.

◆

Academics, including statisticians, are detail obsessives—they need to be. The best can function rather like a camera lens:

looking at the bigger picture one minute, then zooming in on some tiny but significant detail the next. This is a rare and impressive ability—and both Keynes and Kuznets had it. They also had something else in common. Just as Keynes was uncomfortable about expressing his ideas using algebraic symbols for fear of misinterpretation, so, too, Kuznets's earliest writings on national income show his worry about the possible misuse of the work he was doing for the government. Kuznets took pains to explain to his readers that his estimates were an estimate of *incomes* and should not be interpreted as a picture of American economic activity, less still a proxy for economic health.

For the next four decades, Kuznets would complain, writing articles in journals, speaking at conferences. He would argue that, once the war was over, GDP should go back to what it was. He would say that GDP, as currently constructed, was "destined to become one of the most used and misunderstood sources of economic information."[19]

Keynes's relationship to America would always remain complex. He had his critics, including those with whom he was negotiating. Whether during the negotiations over the lend-lease agreements, or later at Bretton Woods, which led to the creation of the World Bank and the International Monetary Fund, anyone on the other side of a conference table experienced the full force of Keynesian pomposity. The British art historian Lord Kenneth Clark, an equally precocious high achiever, recalls a man who did not know how to "dim his headlights."

Kuznets wasn't wrong to believe that a measure of incomes is a far better guide to well-being and to what is important to citizens. But he misjudged the US administration's determination, indeed its insistence, that public spending be included as a positive indicator for economic health. By 1941 Simon Kuznets's days as America's chief national accountant were over. It was Keynes who had effectively helped his younger American colleagues win the argument and defined GDP for generations to come.

Three

Made in Cambridge

I thought that the economics I was taught was insufficiently quantitative and that theory and facts were too widely separated.
—Richard Stone, "The Fortune Teller,"
Economica X (1943)

John Maynard Keynes's role in constructing what eventually became GDP, and his concurrent debate with Simon Kuznets about the place for public spending—the *G* in the GDP formula—has been one of economic history's best-kept secrets. But Keynes wasn't working alone. He had a partner in this endeavor, another of his students and fellow Cambridge economist Richard Stone (1913–1991). After Simon Kuznets, Stone, too, would win a Nobel Prize for his work on national income accounting.[1]

Shortly before his death on April 21, 1946, Keynes persuaded the powers at the University of Cambridge to create a new Department of Applied Economics. Keynes, being Keynes, had a hand in choosing the department's director and ensured that the post would be "for life." Stone was the first director, and the Cambridge department along with Harvard University's Development Advisory Service would together become among the world's leading centers for thinking, teaching, research, and policy advice on macroeconomics. They would incubate the first set of ideas around what GDP would look like, and then help to export them to the four corners of the world.

Although he was among the first generation of Cambridge economists who had studied under Keynes, Richard Stone was unlike his teacher in many ways. He was more of an introvert, altogether more outwardly sensitive, less of a big-picture thinker. Compared with Keynes's very public dramas and on-off relationships with his famous friends,[2] Stone is said by his friends not to have owned a TV or radio. But he did have plenty of inner steel. We know this from his own written account of the time when he clashed with his father over his choice of career. Privately educated, Stone was born to upper-middle-class parents who wanted their son to join one of the moneyed professions; ideally a job in finance or the law would have suited them well. After two years of law Stone switched to economics "much to my father's disappointment," he would write many years later. "At that time the world was in the depth of the Great Depression and my motive for wanting to change subject was the belief, bred of youthful ignorance and optimism, that if only economics was better understood, the world would be a better place."[3]

During the war years, while Keynes was busy negotiating US help for Britain's war effort (the Lend-Lease Act), Stone was working at the British Treasury compiling the country's first official national accounts with the economist James Meade, which would be needed during the talks.

Stone was well aware that the Keynesian template he was working to was out of synch with the Kuznets framework on which the US accounts were based. Had Keynes been in such a position he may well have made some grand statement to a national newspaper, but Stone preferred instead to debate with his US colleagues in the pages of *The Economic Journal*.[4] "What is the economy we wish to measure?" he asked in a 1942 paper, as he urged the United States to include government spending in its accounts. Stone's intervention, along with that of Keynes as we have seen, was just what some of his US counterparts were looking for.

By 1944 civil servants in the US administration had still largely been unsuccessful in shaking off the influence of Simon Kuznets. On their own they needed all the external support they could get. In order to search for a consensus, a three-way meeting was arranged between the UK, the United States, and Canada. Whereas Stone represented the UK, Kuznets had not been invited to represent the US delegation. The result was that the UK's Keynesian proposal to include government spending in the national accounts was adopted by all three nations. This allowed the US economists to break away from Kuznets's definition once and for all and adopt Keynes's definition instead.

Richard Stone was by now developing something of a habit of being in the right place at the right time. Having successfully negotiated the definition of what would become GDP to include government spending, he found himself coming to America's assistance once more. But the results this time would not be so favorable.

◆

With the war over, America was preparing to provide financial aid to Europe. Under what became known as the Marshall Plan, European governments would be given grants and loans at favorable rates to rebuild war-damaged infrastructure. The US government had set up an agency based in Paris called the Organization for European Economic Cooperation. It was the job of the OEEC to monitor how the money was being spent and to check that the funding was helping Europe to become more prosperous—in much the same way that they had earlier sought to measure the effectiveness of President Franklin D. Roosevelt's New Deal policies. To do this, the United States needed to know Europe's existing levels of prosperity. And America's planners figured that the best way to assess the extent of Europe's wealth (or poverty) would be to use the GDP formula. This is how GDP would become a proxy for prosperity.

The OEEC asked Stone to establish an office in Cambridge that would crunch the numbers on the agency's behalf. The OEEC and Stone's suggested prescription was to link America's aid to a European country's GDP. If GDP went up, it meant that the aid was working. If GDP fell, that meant aid was being spent on the wrong things. Later, Stone and his team would train hundreds of economists and statisticians so that in the future each country would do the job for itself.

Europe's countries had no real choice in the matter. If they wanted America's aid, they needed to submit to its system of measurement. Little did they know that the act of measuring their economies would ultimately determine how their economies would be managed. In order to keep receiving American aid, a country's GDP had to go up each year. It meant in practice that the GDP's components needed to go up. In any economy the two easiest things to bump up are government spending and consumer spending, and Europe's economies started to see the size of their public sector get bigger (which is still the case). Something else started to happen: this mainstreaming of GDP would be the start of the idea that national prosperity and GDP are one and the same.

Having embedded GDP across Europe, Stone would soon turn his attention to organizing accounting systems for the rest of the world. The statistics office of the United Nations got in touch and asked him to prepare a template for national accounting, not only for Europe, but for all UN member states. By the late 1950s the system of national accounts developed under Richard Stone had become the gold standard.

When delivering his Nobel lecture in Stockholm in 1984, Richard Stone would pay a generous tribute to his Cambridge University teacher Colin Clark. Clark was Stone's great mentor, and there is no doubt that the two were close. But the reality is that Stone owes as much (if not more) to Keynes. It was Keynes after all who spotted Clark and brought him to Cambridge. It would be Keynes who would give Stone a job as his research assistant when writing *How to Pay for the War*. It was Keynes who recommended Stone to head up the new Department of Applied Economics, from where Stone would introduce GDP to the world. In doing so, perhaps most important of all, Stone used Keynes's definition of GDP, and not that of Colin Clark and Simon Kuznets.

In tapping Stone for the job, Keynes had chosen wisely. He understood that national income accounting needed economists who were good with figures. That sounds like an odd statement to make in today's world, where so much of economics is taught and understood in numerical terms, but in Keynes's day economics was mostly a descriptive field, and economists capable of solving differential equations while taking afternoon tea were thin on the ground. Keynes, himself a mathematics graduate, had spotted Stone's mathematical and statistical abilities.

And yet when it came to the primacy of numbers in policy decisions, the two were different. As we have seen, Keynes was what in today's terms we would call a data-conservative, arguing instead for numerical data to *supplement* human judgment. He believed that it was folly to say with any precision which nations would fight a war or where the next natural disaster or next financial crisis might hit, arguing as he famously did that "in the long run we are all dead."[5] For Keynes, measuring quantities such as factory output or government spending was always an imperfect means to a nobler end. Keynes wanted to count things so that jobs could be created, so that the poorest could escape poverty. Measurement for Keynes was never intended to be an end in itself, and he would urge his colleagues and politicians not to get bogged down in the fog of figures.

Stone, on the other hand, was as much of a theoretician as Keynes but at the same time more of an empiricist, more of a scientist. Theory for Stone was there to be tested with data. He would often claim in interviews that the economics he had been taught was insufficiently quantitative, and that he was no fan of the grand theory that tries to explain everything but with insufficient supporting data—both implicit criticisms of Keynes.[6] And yet, and in spite of his insistence on precision in economics, Stone couldn't see the irony of trying to compress the entire national economy into a single number: GDP.

Throughout his life, Stone would maintain a laser-like focus on national accounts. Honing and refining what goes into the GDP formula and what comes out became his life's obsession and won him the Nobel Prize in 1984. Even if we accept that this was never the intention, Stone and his colleagues helped propagate the idea that GDP, economic growth, and national prosperity are interchangeable. And budding economists from across the world would flock to Cambridge to learn how to work his magic.

Four

The Karachi
Economic Miracle

*Pakistan has had the highest rate of industrial
growth in the world. The only country that comes
close is Japan. Pakistan started out as the hopeless
case. We could not have been more wrong.*
        —Gustav Papanek, "The Development
                        Miracle" (1965)

E lite universities are usually spoiled for choice when it comes
to selecting whom to feature in their alumni magazines.
But there's one University of Cambridge class in particular

that would have left any editor of its alumni magazine *CAM* spoilt for choice.

The economics class of 1953 had Meghnad Desai, now Labour member of the UK House of Lords. It had Nobel Prize-winning economist Amartya Sen, and last but not least, there was Pakistan's Mahbub ul Haq, who would become his country's chief economist and later its finance minister.

I know a tiny bit of this generation, as it is the generation of my own parents: children of the partition of India and participants in what is still the world's largest mass migration. In the late 1940s, members of my own family were debating what to do: whether to stay put in India or to leave for Pakistan. After centuries of coexistence, Hindus, Muslims, and Sikhs found themselves having to choose a new nation and in effect a new identity. India's Muslims and Pakistan's Hindus struggled with the idea of diminished influence. But to migrate meant losing friends, relatives, ending relationships, abandoning homes. And for those who chose to make their new homes in Pakistan, this would be a nation whose very survival was not even certain.[1] This is partly because the new nation was split into two landmasses. West Pakistan housed the capital city, Karachi, and comprised four constituent provinces with their own languages, cultures, and histories. One thousand miles away was East Pakistan, which had a larger population and its own languages. In between lay India. What supposedly united Pakistan's two wings was a shared religion. But we know it wasn't enough, as in 1971 the east broke away to become independent Bangladesh.

In the early 1950s, those who left aboard steam-powered locomotive trains had little more than a few days' food and a change of clothing. On arrival in Pakistan's first capital, Karachi, the refugees would live, sometimes for years, in tented cities. The experience would leave scars, certainly, but also a deep sense of responsibility, not only to themselves and their families, but also to their nations' futures and to the wider cause of prosperity after independence.

◆

That economics class of 1953 would have selected Cambridge, because in the early 1950s the university was at the center of the macroeconomics universe. The connection to Keynes and other leading lights such as Joan Robinson, Richard Kahn, and Richard Stone meant it would attract talented minds keen to absorb the latest ideas and then apply these to a spectrum of economies in the thick of being built (or rebuilt) after the end of World War II. They would become close friends, and yet each of the three would later turn their backs on at least some of what they had learned. Amartya Sen and Mahbub ul Haq would openly revolt against the idea of organizing economies according to GDP. And Haq, an unlikely revolutionary, would lead the design of the United Nations' Human Development Index, which has so far come closest to "dethroning GDP," as one of his longtime associates, Sir Richard Jolly, told me.[2]

Haq died tragically young in 1998. He acknowledged that in his earliest years as an economist he had little time or inclination for economic growth based on anything other than maximizing GDP. "I emerged from the campuses of Cambridge and Yale [with] few doubts about the right path to economic development. Those were happy days. My sights were set. My horizon was clear and there was no hesitancy in my views. I expressed them with a youthful exuberance and conviction which is one of the few privileges of the inexperienced," he wrote in the opening pages of his second book, *The Poverty Curtain*.[3]

◆

But for the early part of his professional life Mahbub ul Haq was a thoroughly mainstream economist. After completing his first degree at Cambridge he headed for the United States, where he took a doctorate at Yale. Returning to Pakistan, he relocated to Karachi, and joined a government body called the Planning Commission, which was tasked with providing a framework through which to run the economy of the newly independent state. Still in his twenties, Haq would be its chief economist.

The Planning Commission's first chairman was Zahid Hussain, a respected intellectual and statesman. In India he had organized the finances of the princely state of Hyderabad. The British writer and historian of India William Dalrymple describes Hyderabad in the 1940s as having an economy the size of Belgium and its ruler's personal fortune running into hundreds of millions of dollars.[4] In February 1937, Hyderabad's ruler was featured on the cover of *Time* magazine as the world's richest man.

In contrast to his life in India, the tasks facing Hussain and his young Pakistani team could not have been more different. For its population of 76 million the new government had to create a currency and banking system; there were taxes to collect, pensions to transfer; electricity, telephone, and postal services had to be organized; road and rail transport had to be established; not to mention finding jobs for the 7 million refugees who had crossed over from the other side. In its first "National Plan," published in 1950, the government planned to build 120 hospitals, 1,200 dispensaries, and 4,460 primary schools. It also set aside $36 million to build institutes for technical training and research labs and to send Pakistanis abroad for higher education.[5]

Pakistan in the early 1950s had few trained economists and few institutions in which to train its up-and-coming talent. Moreover, few of its government officials had experience running the economy of a country, says Gustav Papanek, a development economist based in Boston with extensive experience working in Pakistan at the time.[6]

As relations with Britain were still tense, the Pakistan government chose to approach US-based institutions, including the government, as well as philanthropies such as the Ford Foundation for financial support so that experts from developed countries could be paid to help develop and implement Pakistan's economic plans. The Ford Foundation turned to Harvard University, which sent a team to work alongside government officials in Karachi. Gustav Papanek, who at the age of eighty-eight remains busy advising the governments of developing nations, was one of them. Six decades later, his memory of that period remains vivid.

For Papanek the Harvard assignment had come at just the right time. Then age twenty-five and a socialist, he had lost his job as an economist with the US aid program during Senator Joseph McCarthy's purge of left-wingers from government jobs. "I was the only one who knew about Pakistan in the group," he told me. "When we started there was no economist in the Planning Commission. No one with an economics degree."

With his wife, Hanna Papanek, a sociologist, he moved to Karachi to live from 1954 to 1958. "We were in a newly developed area on Drigh Road among mostly Pakistani families.

There were still many refugee colonies. Small huts with tin roofs," he says, as if explaining something that had happened last week.

◆

Together, Zahid Hussain, Mahbub ul Haq, and the Harvard team took the reins of national planning. And as they did so, those initial priorities to get kids into schools and build 1,200 hospitals gave way to a different style of development model. Instead of building the new nation's health and skills, the planning team decided to go down a development path that emphasized industrial growth.

The National Plan would be modified, with a new focus on developing industry, especially private industry. The promise was self-sufficiency in food, 2 million more jobs, and a 60 percent increase in industrial output. To achieve these goals, 28 percent of spending would go to industrial projects, as opposed to the 11 percent earmarked for farming. In contrast, what the government pejoratively called "social services," including health, education, and housing, would be allocated far less. The government's new advisers were basically saying that developing countries had to get rich first through industrialization before they could spend. Schools would get 4 percent of public spending and health care even less: just 2 percent.[7]

What Haq called "growth philosophy" meant resisting demands to invest in health and housing. "During the industrial revolution, no one gave much thought to the emergence of slums, the prevalence of bad sanitary conditions and the need for social security benefits for the aged, the needy and the sick," Haq would write.[8] Instead, the bedrock of growth philosophy was to develop private industry (maximizing the I in the GDP formula).

Except that the planners had a problem. "There was no industry to speak of," says Papanek. At the time of partition in 1947, 1.4 million owners of businesses left to join India, including the bulk of large businesses. Fewer than 300,000 traders moved the other way.[9] Even in agriculture, although Pakistani farmers were among the world's largest exporters of cotton and jute, practically all of the cotton and jute textile mills were now over the new border with India.

As Papanek recalls, the focus in those initial years was to find and build big businesses. New industries such as cement manufacturing, or new industrial facilities such as cotton mills, needed new industrialists. And as most had left for India, the Karachi government and its Harvard advisers had to find ways to make some of the city's small-scale trading families into owners of much larger businesses. Had this been a question for today, the answer might have been to deregulate, so that many more people could try out their business ideas. But instead the government sought to do the opposite: by restricting competition, it effectively handpicked the companies that would be allowed to grow. That meant a handful of chosen families were effectively given a license to print money. The result was that industrial production increased at a greater rate than had been forecast. It also made a relatively small number of people into the new superrich.

Meanwhile, although the Planning Commission chairman, Zahid Hussain, had promised that spending on health, education, and housing could not happen at the same time as spending on GDP-style economic development,[10] in practice a government that had to be reelected couldn't entirely ignore the scale of poverty literally on its doorstep. Public spending on housing and education did increase slightly between 1955 and 1960, though this was concentrated on universities and on housing for the middle classes. On the other hand, health and welfare spending fell to even lower levels than had been forecast.[11]

GDP had grown at a modest 2.5 percent.[12] At the end of their first five-year experiment at pulling Pakistan's people out of poverty by ramping up one of the components of GDP, Pakistan's planners were none too satisfied.

◆

GDP growth of 2.5 percent was pretty poor, and so by the time Mahbub ul Haq had arrived in the Planning Commission, thinking had begun on the next five-year plan, which would take the country from 1960 to 1965.[13] The planners stuck to their formula, again focusing most of the spending on farming and industry; with education, health, and welfare altogether occupying only 7 percent of the budget.[14]

The medicine worked, in that GDP duly increased by around 6 percent for the period of the second plan, from 1960 to 1965, with manufacturing growing by more than twice that rate.[15] The young economists basked in the glow of fame and were tasked with preparing a third plan, largely along the same lines as the first two, although this time with a larger share given to social services.

Pakistan was seen around the world as a model economy which merited a visit from no less than President Dwight D. Eisenhower. America had helped to pay to house many refugees, but Papanek recalls that when Eisenhower flew into Karachi for a state visit in 1959, he was advised not to get too close to the refugee settlements.[16] "Instead the president was taken in a low flying plane. I always wondered how much he realized the misery of the people below."

"Growth had created jobs, which helped the poor, and it showed that economic incentives work," Papanek said in a speech in New York in May 1965, which he called "The Development Miracle." He added, "Pakistan has had the highest rate of industrial growth in the world. The only country that comes close is Japan. Output of industry is increasing 14 percent or so per year, which is really quite remarkable. Pakistan started out as *the* hopeless case. We could not have been more wrong."[17]

As to the lowly sums spent on health and education, Haq was clear. "The road to eventual equalities may inevitably lie through initial inequalities," he would later reflect.[18] "Economic growth is a brutal, sordid process. There are no short cuts to it. The essence of it lies in making the labourer produce more than he is allowed to consume for his immediate needs." He added, "The first priority was growth; the other issues had to take a secondary place. The commitment to a growth philosophy was so wholehearted that all other policies were subordinated to it."

◆

And yet Haq and his advisers could also see that the raw numbers were masking a more complex picture.

Several problems stood out: First, GDP growth rates in the east were lower than in the west, especially in manufacturing, which was concentrated in the west. Second, as we've seen, the original National Plan's priorities to build hospitals and schools had been torn up.

Third, the lack of a minimum wage and controls on trade unions meant there was no external incentive to enable wages to keep pace with inflation, which was leading to strikes. The main beneficiaries of the industrial boom seemed to be the middle and upper classes, as they were the only ones who could afford to live in the new houses being built and buy the new consumer goods that were being produced by Pakistan's newly minted industrial families.

Fourth, and tucked away in the data tables, was one quite troubling statistic. Foreign aid and loans had trebled to about $3 billion during the five years of the second plan. This amounted to around half the government's bill for spending on agriculture and industry and suggested that the industrial boom was more precarious than it looked.[19] What would happen, for example, if international assistance were to fluctuate, which it had done for much of Pakistan's history?

Perhaps most worrying of all for Haq was the policy that allowed only a small number of families to become superrich by preventing other businesses from competing with them, in contrast to the original National Plan, which had recognized that new businesses needed access to capital in order to grow.[20] After nearly a decade of a policy that Haq called "Functional Inequality," he had begun to seriously question it.

Mahbub ul Haq could now see that his dogged focus on growth had done little to help the mass of citizens become healthier or better educated. He knew that there was little state protection for someone who became ill or unemployed. He could see that unemployment remained stubbornly high, and its effects he witnessed firsthand when trade unions started agitating for strike action. Moreover, he could see that concentrating wealth in a small number of families was acting as a brake on competition and stopping others from establishing their own firms.

And so on a spring morning in April 1968, a chastened Mahbub ul Haq took to the lectern at a management convention in Karachi. His audience of policy makers and members of the newly created West Pakistan Management Association might have been anticipating a speech that would celebrate continuous economic growth and Pakistan's new status as a third world exemplar. But Haq, who did not have a prepared text, began by apologizing to his hosts if he sounded rambling. In a sign of what was to come, he asked that his remarks be taken not as those of the Planning Commission's chief economist, but as those of "an ordinary economist to fellow professionals on the critical issues of our time."[21]

The speech began in a familiar vein. Haq started off by recounting the successes, including economic growth of more than 6 percent and more than 5 million new jobs. But then the narrative changed. Haq's wife, Khadija, a fellow economist, had been looking at data from the Karachi Stock Exchange and had discovered that just twenty families owned 66 percent of industrial companies, 79 percent of insurance funds, and 80 percent of banks listed on the exchange.[22] Those families, Haq noted in his speech, had a responsibility to invest their largesse on behalf of a growing nation. And then came what sounded like a call to civil disobedience. If the newly wealthy weren't able to act more responsibly, he said, then "society has every right, in fact it has the duty, to resist the emergence of a privileged class of entrepreneurs which is pampered by fiscal concessions, which is sheltered by prohibitive tariffs, which is nurtured by artificial incentives and which makes its living on the basis of imperfect and inefficient competition."[23]

Here was the government's own chief economist drilling holes in a whole decade's worth of his own policies. He was saying that Pakistan's twenty newly industrial families had gotten rich on the back of public money and they were now hoarding wealth when they should be investing it or redistributing it. The speech, not surprisingly, became an overnight sensation.

Haq's speech stunned both ordinary citizens and opinion formers, including the political and landowning classes, as well as those living in the handsome military colonies. Arguments ensued about the size of the list and who should—and shouldn't—be on it. Nearly a decade earlier Gustav Papanek had calculated that some twenty-four families controlled half of all industrial assets.[24] Some years later the economist Lawrence White expanded the list to forty-three family groups.[25] But few argued with Haq's basic point: that countries do not become more prosperous if government policies focus on stopping all but a small number of wealth creators from becoming ever richer.

◆

Mahbub ul Haq was not alone in discovering firsthand the damage that could be done by managing an economy through a narrow focus on GDP. Five thousand miles west of Karachi, another Cambridge alumnus had come to the same conclusion. This was Dudley Seers, inspirational statistician, founder of the Institute of Development Studies based at the University of Sussex, and an adviser to the then British Labour government of Harold Wilson and especially Wilson's minister for overseas development, the formidable Barbara Castle.

Seers, who died at age sixty-three in 1983, has now been largely written out of economic histories, but according to those who knew him, he seems to have been no less exciting to work for than Keynes. Seers had a "quality of rock-like independence, which was inspiring," recalled his colleague Paul Streeten. "When Dudley entered a room, without saying or doing anything, just quietly slipping into his place, somehow the temperature, the alertness, and the level of excitement rose."[26]

During the 1960s Seers had been traveling the length and breadth of Britain's newly independent former colonies, advising their governments on strategies to reduce poverty. He watched as countries such as Kenya and Zambia established national statistical offices, sometimes paid for by the aid programs of richer governments. And he despaired when discovering they had to implement a GDP-focused system that measured things that didn't matter much to their people's prosperity. Seers heard accounts from the directors of these offices, who complained that their governments would often pressure them to show GDP always on the rise, and he heard about the often questionable data on which GDP figures were being compiled in some places. Decimal points in a developing country's GDP are a "fantasy," Seers famously said in a 1969 lecture entitled "What Are We Trying to Measure?"[27] Seers reflected many of Haq's experiences. He said: "What has been happening to poverty? What has been happening to unemployment? What has been happening to inequality? If one or two of these central problems have been growing worse, especially if all three have, it would be strange to call the result 'development,' even if per capita income has soared."

The GDP index, he reminded his audience, had been created to suit the needs of countries *that had already developed*. Few OECD member states, for example, had become prosperous by sticking to the GDP formula. Few had become rich by increasing consumption and giving the private sector a free hand. Countries such as America and Britain, Seers said, had chosen to implement GDP only after absolute poverty had been eliminated; only after unemployment was at historically low levels; and only after these countries had felt that inequality was in retreat. Developing countries, Seers observed in his lecture, should be encouraged to do so too.

For all the force of his argument, it seems that Seers understood that his speech had made little headway with policy makers. There was no change to the GDP-focused policies of international development funders that Seers knew well, nor any change to the GDP requirements of statistics offices in developing countries.

And so Seers chose a different approach. He organized an international meeting in which the aim was to gather together the heads of the statistics offices in developing countries with the representatives of the donor agencies, all in the same room. The meeting lasted a week and took place in Sussex (rather than London), which minimized the chances of people leaving early.

The government statisticians explained how they were caught in a tug-of-war. On the one side there was pressure from heads of government to make the figures look good, even if that meant falsifying data. On the other side was pressure from international agencies, including the UN, to measure things that had little relevance to national or local needs, and which often had the effect of distorting reality. For example, many newly independent but poor countries appeared wealthier because of high military budgets. If that wasn't enough, they repeated, international technical experts weren't really helping, as they were paid to carry out, rather than question, the orders they were given by donor governments. "The more a statistical office relies on technical assistance," Seers remarked, "the more it has to accept the priorities of donors."

The meeting, as its report makes clear, was not a particularly happy affair. Representatives from the international agencies, who included Richard Stone, tried to defend themselves by saying that the GDP template should not be treated as if it was some immutable law. But Seers, though hosting the event, was unequivocal. "What statistics we use mould our perception of reality," he said, bringing the meeting to a close. "This is why such a dull subject is crucially important."[28]

Seers was a creative thinker with a sense of fun. And as a statistician he wasn't so much against GDP as in favor of amending it to measure the things that matter. Richard Jolly, one of his former students and later director at the Institute of Development Studies at Sussex, recalls that Seers once said that a "shoe index" would be more useful than GDP as a measure of prosperity for the poorest countries.[29] Such an index would count four things: the numbers of people who walked barefoot; the number who wore shoes with soles made from recycled car tires; the number who wore locally manufactured leather shoes; and finally, the number who wore imported shoes from companies such as Bata. The point he was trying to make was that data is of use to policy makers only if it is (a) relevant and (b) useful in the sense that making a change will actually improve people's lives in a discernible way.

❖

Dudley Seers and Mahbub ul Haq were early critics of a blunt, data-driven approach to creating and measuring prosperity. Haq's 1968 speech changed the language of politics and economics and introduced the phrase "the twenty-two families," which many in South Asia still use today, nearly a half century later, as a proxy for wealth concentration and abuse of privilege.[30] It changed his life, too, in that it planted a seed for his efforts to challenge economic policy making that is fixated on rising GDP. And it paved the way for the Human Development Index, although that would happen two decades later.

Shortly after the "twenty-two families" speech, Pakistan became engulfed in yet another political crisis that would end a decade-long military rule, paving the way for the country's next experiment with democracy. Haq, however, chose not to stay, crossing the Atlantic for a new and in many ways more influential job as head of policy and planning at the World Bank in Washington, DC. He would work under Robert McNamara, President John F. Kennedy's controversial secretary for defense during the Vietnam War.

While at the World Bank, Haq would retain a strong interest in what he called the "sins of development planners," and it would be in Washington that he would write *The Poverty Curtain*, a reflection on his decade as Pakistan's chief economic adviser. "Brazil has recently achieved a growth rate of close to 7 percent but persisting mal-distribution of income continues to threaten the very fabric of its society. What has gone wrong?" he would ask. "We were confidently told that if you take care of your [GDP], poverty will take care of itself. We were often reminded to keep our eyes focused on a high growth target, as it was the best guarantee of eliminating unemployment and of redistributing incomes. Then what really happened?"[31]

In Washington, Haq would continue to play an important role in the emergent discussions about GDP alternatives. However, as we shall see in Chapter 7, this role would not quite be the one he was expecting.

Five

Red Star Over Central Square

> *In a city like Cambridge, red areas aren't about*
> *home cooking, gun-toting and moral values-loving.*
> — *The Harvard Crimson*, December 9, 2004

A t 550 Massachusetts Avenue in Cambridge, Massachusetts, a narrow doorway transports the visitor to what feels like a contradiction wrapped in a time-warp. A few minutes from Central Square subway station, less than a mile each way from the campuses of Harvard and MIT, is the Center for

Marxist Education. When I popped in for a visit in 2018, the interior seemed like it had changed little from when it was first established in the 1970s. Its walls were adorned with posters of Marx and Lenin, its red curtains emblazoned with the hammer and sickle. Visitors still came for periodic talks on topics such as "The US Cold War on China" and to borrow books from its library of communist and Marxist literature.

Cambridge is among America's most left-leaning cities—90 percent of those who voted in the 2020 elections cast their ballots for Joe Biden and Kamala Harris.[1] That it is, is because of a longer history of radical politics. In the years after the end of World War II, many of the city's residents, including academics from the two universities, believed genuinely that communism offered a fairer model to rebuild societies, compared with capitalism. They would meet at places like the Center for Marxist Education. And tragically, many hundreds, if not thousands, suffered consequences that would affect them for the rest of their lives.

From the early 1950s to the 1960s, the US government used every means at its disposal—legal and illegal—to flush out and punish America's communists. Laws were passed that made it illegal to be a communist, and the Federal Bureau of Investigation launched one of the biggest instances of state-sponsored mass surveillance that 20th-century America had ever seen. Neighbours spied on neighbours. Employers—including universities—handed lists to the government of people they thought were communists. Passports were taken away so people could not leave.[2] The instigator was the infamous Senator Joseph McCarthy. But in reality, the hunt for communists in America involved practically every organ of the state—from the White House, to members of Congress, the Federal Bureau of Investigation (FBI), even the courts.

Infiltration was the US government's biggest concern—lawmakers believed that America's communists were taking their orders from Moscow. There's good evidence that some were, says Yeshiva University's Ellen Schrecker, the doyenne of the historians of the McCarthy period. But the overwhelming majority were simply regular people, looking for what they thought was a better way to achieve racial and economic justice. And large numbers of those who found themselves caught in the McCarthy net were not even communists—including Gustav Papanek.

Gustav Papanek's politics were not in the least communist—he describes himself as a democratic socialist. But that didn't matter to the Eisenhower administration. Papanek's family roots went back to central Europe. His father had been involved in left-wing politics in Austria before the family fled to the United States at the beginning of the 20th century. And Papanek himself had been a member of student socialist societies while at university. That was enough for the government's communist hunters to put him on the blacklist. The government initially tried to have Papanek fired from his job working in the State Department, but realized that wasn't possible as he had worked for the US military during World War II. This gave him what is called Veterans Protection and meant he couldn't be dismissed from a government job.[3]

"What [the president] General Eisenhower did was to simply abolish our agency," Papanek explained. The Eisenhower administration then created a new agency with a different name and hired 85 per cent of the staff of the old agency back, Papanek says. "But they didn't hire back those they considered incompetent, or communists. So I was one of the people who received notification that my services were being terminated."

Newly jobless, and with a family to support, Papanek called up his old Harvard colleagues to see if they could help him find work—ideally outside of the United States. "To my amazement I found that Harvard was putting together a team of economic advisers to go to Pakistan."[4] This was the famous Harvard Development Advisory Service, where Mahbub ul Haq would learn his trade as a growth architect, and where Papanek, blacklisted at home, would spend the next 60 years in a career at the centre of America's international anti-communism crusade.

◆

America's purge of those it considered to be communists was of course not restricted to its own borders. It competed with the Soviet Union to influence, if not control, the countries of the developing world that were becoming free from European colonialism. Both Moscow and Washington sent eye-watering amounts of aid, and shipped expensive weapons to support military dictatorships, so that countries could come round to their way of thinking and acting.

Promoting economic growth was one (albeit small) part of America's mission to destroy communism. And in that mission, there was one economist who towered above all others. This was Walt Whitman Rostow, a gifted, ambitious, personable, yet ruthless economic historian from the Massachusetts Institute of Technology (MIT) who served Presidents John F. Kennedy and Lyndon Johnson as an adviser on national security.

Rostow was in the group of high-flyers in the Kennedy White House that the journalist David Halberstam tagged as "The Best and the Brightest" in his book of that name.[5] Just a few years before taking the White House job in 1961, Rostow had climbed his way from obscurity to become one of the world's most recognizable economists, and famous for his idea that communism could be defeated through growth—and violence. His biographer, the historian David Milne calls him "a missionary imperialist."

Like other members of the cast of this book, Walt Whitman Rostow was born in the first decades of the 20th century to Jewish parents who had left Eastern Europe for the United States. He was raised initially in Brooklyn, but at the age of 16, when most teens are still finishing high school, Rostow won a scholarship to attend Yale University in 1932. It was a decision that would set the course of his professional and intellectual life. At Yale, Rostow met fellow economist Max Millikan, who would later bring him to MIT. And it was at Yale that Rostow became obsessed with the ideas of Karl Marx. Never short of self-belief, he vowed one day to match the communist thinker for global influence.[6]

To an extent, Rostow shared Marx's desire to help the poor to live more prosperous and fulfilling lives. Marx wanted citizens to seize control of the means of production, ushering in the communist revolution where ownership would be shared between people, and where there would be equality of income, wealth, and opportunity.[7] Rostow could see how Marx's ideas would appeal to countries fighting liberation struggles against colonial powers, and so he came up with his own "non-communist manifesto"—that being the subtitle given to his bestselling *Stages of Economic Growth*,[8] part three of a trilogy of books on growth.[9] In *Stages* Rostow claimed to have found the formula, the elixir through which any poor country could become as prosperous as Europe or America. All it needed to do was to follow Rostow's five-stage prescription. For Rostow, investing in technology and large quantities of capital spending were among the keys to a society taking off. Capital and 'take-off' were terms he would return to again and again during the course of his career.

◆

So what were Rostow's five stages? A country in the first stage of growth would be a traditional or largely rural/agricultural society, lacking the know-how to develop modern science at scale, or the means to similarly manipulate its environment for human benefit. To escape from this stage, a country needed to put in place measures that would allow it to take off into industrial growth. For Rostow, countries were ready to take off when they could afford to increase the share of capital investment—the I in the GDP formula—from 5 percent to 10 percent of national income.[10]

Rostow's ideas on how this could be achieved included moving workers out of low-paying rural and agricultural jobs, and into higher-paying consumer industries. He urged countries to put a stop to feudalism (as had happened in Europe), and allow all citizens equal rights to own land and property, run their own businesses, and patent or trademark their inventions and innovations. He called for big investments in science, technology, universities and industry, partly so that more countries could create global corporations, just as America had done.

The first edition of *Stages* includes a hand-drawn graphic of countries, categorized according to their place on Rostow's scale. Britain, according to Rostow, experienced its take-off in the final decades before 1800. For America, take-off happened somewhere between 1845 and 1860. For Germany, it was 1850 to 1870. China and India, according to Rostow, were ready to take off in 1959 and he predicted that, by 2020, both countries would become consumer societies and advanced technological powers.

Rostow's fifth and final stage was what he called a society of "high mass consumption." Rostow was slightly obsessed with car ownership data and *Stages* concludes with a table that compares the number of private cars in seven countries, starting with the United States and ending with Russia. In 1900, America is listed as having 8,000 cars, France 3,000. By 1957, America had ascended to 56 million cars according to Rostow's calculations, whereas Russia languished at 415,000.[11] The message, in case anyone had forgotten, was that communism keeps you poor, while industrial capitalism makes you rich. Europe and America had successfully fought off communism to create high standards of living for their citizens, and in retracing their footsteps Rostow had prepared the road map for other nations to follow.

◆

Stages was published on April 8, 1960. It was an instant publishing sensation. A day later, *The Bookseller* reported that a reprint was already underway as hardback copies would be sold out by the end of the month. The book, which was widely reviewed in both the specialist and the mass media, achieved that rare feat of uniting reviewers of the centre, left and right. *The New York Times*'s positive review was published under the headline "How to compete with the Russians". *The Economist* published a 16-page summary of *Stages*, which it called "one of the most stimulating contributions made to economic and political thought since the war."[12] Even the right-wing *New York Post*'s syndicated columnist Max Lerner was no less impressed, marveling, as so many reviewers did, at the simplicity of Rostow's five-step plan to modernity. "Anyone who has been in Asia or the Middle East recently will bear witness that the term most frequently on the lips of the planners is 'take-off'," Lerner wrote. "It is as if they want to jump, by a single leap, from their traditional economy and society of yesterday straight into the 1960s. And while they take the leap they want a blueprint to read." Rostow's blueprint was, for Lerner, exactly what was needed to keep communism at bay. "Independence from colonialism need not lead to enslavement at the hands of a new imperialism," he gushed.[13]

The Financial Times, meanwhile, chose Roy Harrod, a contemporary and biographer of John Maynard Keynes, and himself a distinguished growth economist, to review the book. Harrod could not contain his pride that Rostow had decreed Britain to be the first country to achieve take-off. "No British patriot can feel sore at any lack of recognition in this book," he wrote—though Harrod still chided his American colleague for not giving more weight to the role of "innate British character," which had helped Britain to export the rule of law, democracy, and universities all over the world.[14]

Rostow's formula for how nations could prosper without going communist also attracted VIP fan mail. His admirers included President Eisenhower and the more stridently anti-communist vice-president, Richard Nixon. This was all the more remarkable as Nixon was a critic of managing economies through growth, and would taunt Kennedy as a "growth-man" during the 1960 presidential election campaign.[15] Nixon wrote to Rostow congratulating him and saying he planned to use some of Rostow's arguments during an upcoming visit to Moscow.[16]

That is not to say that everyone was impressed. *Stages* had its fair share of critics, too—not least, of course, the Soviet media, which could not allow a bestseller with the subtitle "A

Non-Communist Manifesto" to pass without comment. In October, a lengthy and sarcastic response appeared in *Pravda*, the Soviet Communist Party's daily newspaper, in which Rostow was denounced as "a market-place magician" and his ideas ridiculed as "bourgeois propaganda".[17] *Pravda*'s review came just weeks after Soviet leader Nikita Khrushchev's had boasted to American audiences during a two-week visit that Soviet rates of growth were "three to five times" as high as those in America.[18]

But away from the propaganda and point-scoring, Soviet economists and statisticians had reacted much more carefully to the book. They regarded Rostow as a serious scholar, someone to engage with, and Rostow was invited by the prestigious Academy of Sciences of the Soviet Union to present his ideas. The Academy would have needed top-level clearance to do this, which suggests that the Soviet leadership, too, wanted to hear and see Rostow in person. He traveled to Leningrad and Moscow between May 19 and 26, 1959, accompanied by his wife Elspeth, also an academic at MIT. From his notes of the visit and subsequent correspondence with US colleagues, it's clear that Rostow was excited about the trip: he relished the prospect of argument and debate.[19] But it's also striking from his letters that Rostow was much less bombastic about defeating communism. In fact, his main talk in Moscow was called "The Stages of Economic Growth and the Problems of Peaceful Co-Existence"—a title he had been given by his hosts. Writing to his MIT colleagues, Rostow said he was "anxious not to convey any sense that morally, Americans as people were any better than Russians as people"—a very different tone to the more aggressive "how to defeat communism" flavour of Rostow's own articles, and the many reviews of *Stages* in newspapers and magazines.

Rostow was asked by his hosts what he thought about the

Soviet economy's size and growth rate—specifically, if he thought it was a third or a half of that of the United States.[20] The question underscored how Soviet academics did not believe their government's official statistics. Rostow answered that the Soviet economy was likely a half of that of the United States, which was confirmed by subsequent studies.[21]

He was also asked how the United States could be classified as a consumer society when there was evidence of inequality and high levels of poverty and unemployment, especially in the country's more rural, inland parts. Rostow seemed to struggle to answer this credibly. Rostow was also told that Soviet economists were increasingly adopting more quantitative methods and producing economic analysis based on data and models. He called this a dangerous trend, partly, he said, because models are only as good as the data fed into them. "The danger," Rostow claimed, was that "young men would get so absorbed in the fascinations of the methods and the problems within the method that they would forget what problems the methods were supposed to help solve." And he revealed a scepticism of GDP as a measure, which he said was not a good way to capture quality of life—he called it "the numbers racket approach."

It was a successful visit, Rostow wrote excitedly in his letters back home. The Rostows invited their Soviet hosts for a return visit to America, and the goodwill was reciprocated. A young Russian graduate student assigned to look after their travel needs—whom Rostow referred to as "Lubimov"—said: "We disagreed, but it's so important that we have met and looked at one another over and over. And then we said we hoped to meet again. It must happen. It must happen."

◆

Rostow's status as a bestselling author, and his near-celebrity reception among Moscow's intellectuals, contrasted with what was awaiting him back in the universities of the United States and Western Europe. By the standards of scholarship, *Stages* had insufficient data or supporting references. Most other academics might well have been dismissed for claiming to have produced a global prescription for how to grow an economy in 137 pages, but Rostow had too many friends in high places to be ignored. This presented his fellow economists—and particularly the profession's leaders—with something of a headache. But their professional trade body, the International Economic Association, came up with a novel solution: it organized a conference devoted to just one topic—Rostow and *Stages*. Rostow would be accorded the importance he felt he deserved; his peers, meanwhile, would have their day in court.

The conference took place in Konstanz, then in West Germany. Anyone who was anyone in academic economics seemed to have been invited. There was GDP's co-creator Simon Kuznets; the historian of the British industrial revolution, Phyllis Deane; and the growth theorist Robert Solow. It must have been quite an event, though evidently not a happy one. Kuznets summed up the overall mood of his colleagues, calling *Stages* "a heroic over-simplification." In response, Rostow called the judgment of his peers "an act of aggression."[22]

The economists had come prepared, and immediately went on the attack. They queried why Rostow had neglected—whether deliberately or otherwise—to define, precisely, what he meant by the terms he was using, as not doing so made it hard to test or replicate his conclusions. They asked why he had failed or refused to explain how a country's progress through the stages of economic growth could be measured. Apart from a handful of countries mentioned in the book, the absence of a measure made it impossible for all other countries to know what stage they were in, or if they were ready for take-off.

Rostow was no fan of growth indicators such as GDP, as we've seen from his remarks in Moscow. But he did write in *Stages* that countries needed to satisfy three conditions for take-off, the first condition being that the country increase its investment from "say" 5 percent to 10 percent of national income. The second condition was that at least one industrial manufacturing sector should be developed to "a high rate of growth"—though he neglected to say what he meant by that. Rostow's third condition, and arguably the most difficult measure, was that take-off needed "a political, social and institutional framework." This likely meant that countries needed to find ways to mobilize the required capital.[23] Later, Rostow would advocate foreign aid for less developed nations as a source of capital investment, but this wasn't evident in the first edition of *Stages* which his peers were about to tear apart.

Prior to the conference the economists had set themselves the task of calculating take-off in a number of countries based on two out of Rostow's three conditions, using some assumptions. First, Kuznets assumed that Rostow was measuring growth using national income accounting, or a version of GDP. Second, to measure Rostow's idea of the "take-off", Kuznets assumed that Rostow was advocating a doubling of capital investment—the I in the GDP formula—as a proportion of national income.

As noted, Phyllis Deane, the leading authority on the history of British economic growth and the industrial revolution, was present at the event. The organizers had asked her to test Rostow's data on Britain. Deane, a colleague of Richard Stone at the University of Cambridge, estimated that capital investment in

England and Wales was around 6.5 percent of national income between 1780 and 1800. At first glance this seemed to correspond to Rostow's dates for the British take-off (1783 to 1802). It also wasn't far off his estimate of investment as 5 percent of national income. From the 1820s to the 1850s, Deane calculated that British capital investment went up by 9 percent; and increased again to 14 percent in the decade before the start of World War I in 1914.

Deane next compared Britain's increase in capital investment with its rates of economic growth—the other side of the Rostow equation. British growth rates were 1.5 percent during Rostow's take-off period of 1780 to 1800, rising to 2.5 percent toward the end of the 1800s.[24] These rates were not spectacular, but we need to remember that Rostow did not accept GDP as his growth measure of choice for a take-off—that was Kuznets' decision.

It was a broadly similar story for Germany, where, according to Rostow, take-off happened between 1850 and 1873. The Konstanz meeting chose the University of Munster's Walther Hoffmann to review Rostow's Germany data, and Hoffmann found that capital investment was 8.5 percent for the 1850s; it was 9.75 percent for the 1860s, and 13.5 percent for the 1870s—again, not that far off from Rostow's projected doubling. But Germany's growth was a much more anaemic 2.5 percent throughout the three decades from 1851 to 1880.[25]

Kuznets concluded that Rostow was right to study how economies grow and industrialize, but that he was wrong to think that he was studying observable reality. Instead of "take-off", he advised his colleague to use the more accurate term, "early phase of modern economic growth". Robert Solow was just as scathing. He said as the meeting was winding up how he had felt throughout the conference "that take-off in any country occurred when Professor Rostow felt that it had occurred."

Rostow reiterated that growth—as measured using the GDP formula—is not capable of accurately capturing how economies are progressing during and after take-off. He reminded Kuznets that the future Nobel laureate, of all people, should know this argument, as Kuznets himself had made it in earlier years. "The point takes on a certain drama because, in my early education, I derived much from the early work of Professor Kuznets," Rostow proclaimed.

Although clearly frustrated, Rostow didn't seem to mind tolerating his academic colleagues' opprobrium, so long as the letters and phone calls from heads of government and influential newspaper editors kept coming—which they did. In fact, by the time of the conference, Rostow had already netted what would be his biggest political catch of all—a young senator named John F. Kennedy who was eyeing up a bid to become the next US president.

◆

It's unusual, even today, for a university academic to enjoy Rostowian levels of access to the top level of American government. But in Rostow's case, such an outcome was not an accident. He deliberately cultivated powerful people and institutions, and was helped in no small measure by his university, the Massachusetts Institute of Technology. For most of the early part of his career, Rostow was a professor at MIT's Center for International Studies (CENIS). This was a policy think tank created in 1951 by the university's leadership to help the US government find solutions to problems needing research expertise—especially in its efforts to defeat the Soviet Union in the Cold War. The center's first project—Project Troy—involved MIT engineers researching how to stop the Soviet Union from jamming the Voice of America radio signals that were being beamed into Eastern Europe.[26]

For most of its first 18 years, the MIT center was led by Rostow's friend from his Yale days, the economist Max Millikan, and Millikan was just as ambitious as Rostow. Both had worked for the research division of Allied intelligence during World War II. Rostow's role had been to help the military pick bombing targets in Germany, and that experience gave the pair an insight into how governments and their decision-makers use research. Policy makers often want fast answers to complex questions, and many like to be told things in black and white. They tend not to like the language of uncertainty, caveats and error bars, which is how academics commonly communicate among themselves. Researchers act in this way because they know that rushed or overly confident research can be bad science, and that decisions based on bad science can have serious and potentially dangerous consequences. But Millikan and Rostow were prepared to adapt and change if it meant they could influence those in power. If policy makers wanted research to be done quickly, and if they wanted to be told what to think, then Millikan and Rostow were ready to deliver.

One of the center's first outputs was a book, *Dynamics of Soviet Society*, which was published in 1953.[27] But a lot of other work from that early period remains classified because the center's first funder was the Central Intelligence Agency—a decision that the university's leadership would later regret. The CIA provided $1 million (equivalent to about $10 million in 2020) for its first two years. Visitors to MIT's Sloan Building on Memorial

Drive in Cambridge, where the center was located overlooking the Charles River, would be greeted by a security guard—and its office space included a restricted area containing a vault for classified documents.

Millikan and the MIT leadership had initially wanted the State Department to come on board, but the department declined, afraid that its involvement with MIT would attract yet more unwelcome attention from McCarthy, the FBI and the US Congress's various anti-communist committees. The university itself was under intense scrutiny as, in the MIT center's founding year, one of its top mathematicians, Dirk Struik, had been splashed all over the national news after being indicted, wrongly, for indoctrinating students with communism.

But the CIA had less, if any, hesitation toward paying the bills, so long as MIT's researchers were happy to help the agency find answers to questions. For its first task, Millikan and Rostow were asked by their sponsors for a study on the Soviet Union's weak points—presumably so that the US could focus its Cold War efforts in places where it could do the most damage. The pair set to work with a team of America's academic experts on the Soviet Union. Within 18 months of being commissioned, a classified version of *Dynamics of Soviet Society* was on the desk of CIA director Allen Dulles. For Rostow and Millikan, the timing of their report couldn't have been better. When Josef Stalin died in March 1953, the pair were summoned to the White House to brief President Eisenhower's advisors. They recommended that the United States should provide communist countries, and those close to the orbit of communism, with economic development assistance—they also recommended reunifying Germany and ending the Korean War. Injecting large amounts of capital would help these countries to grow, and at the same time weaken their links to the Soviet Union, they argued. As we have seen, this same formula would later find its way into the pages of *Stages of Economic Growth*.

That first report also provided Rostow and Millikan with an early lesson in policy advice: they will have realized that being in the same room as decision-makers is not enough to have impact—policy makers need to be confident that they can trust the messenger, as much as the message. And here, the duo had a problem: not only did parts of the Eisenhower administration think MIT and Harvard harboured communists, but many Republicans were also opposed to what they called "growth-manship" (as seen in Nixon's "growth-man" dismissal of Kennedy, referenced earlier). Economists close to the Republicans didn't agree that providing capital injections, let alone tuning an entire economy according to $C + I + G$, would lead to prosperity. And Republican policy makers also, rightly, associated such an approach with their political opponents in the previous administrations of Franklin Delano Roosevelt and Harry Truman.[28] So while the CIA continued to fund the MIT Center—it clearly liked what it was hearing—the US administration itself was less on board with what Rostow and Millikan were proposing. It would in fact take another eight years and the arrival of Kennedy for their message to get through.

By the time *Stages* appeared in the late 1950s, John F. Kennedy was building his own personal think tank ahead of a future run for the White House—which is how he met Rostow. David Halberstam, in *The Best and the Brightest*, said Rostow was a "demon for work," always available when summoned by the Senator. "When Kennedy wanted a memo on some subject, Rostow did not, as too many academics did, refer him to some piece of paper they had already written."[29] By the time of the

1960 election, Rostow and Millikan had become a fixture on Kennedy's campaign team—Rostow even came up with Kennedy's election slogan: "Let's get America moving again." Through their writings, and their advocacy, the pair helped persuade Kennedy that US economic and military aid could be harnessed to serve the goals of economic growth and anti-communism. With Kennedy victorious, Rostow was virtually guaranteed a job in the new administration—except that it would not be on the Treasury team, nor with the Council of Economic Advisers. Instead, Kennedy put Rostow in the White House as one of his advisers on national security, which included responsibility for defence and security policy in Asia. That seems like an odd choice for someone with a 20-year record of writing and research in economics—but in hindsight, it made perfect sense.

◆

Gustav Papanek remembers encountering Walt Whitman Rostow at an airport in the early 1950s when the MIT Center for International Studies was still largely working under contract to the CIA and the Ford Foundation, the philanthropic arm of the mighty Ford Motor Company. Rostow was returning to the US, and Papanek was on his way back to Karachi, working under a separate Ford-funded economic assistance project. It must have been quite a surreal encounter, as, before then, the two had never met. "I asked him, 'What are you doing these days?'," Papanek recalls. Rostow, according to Papanek, said he had been to Indonesia for three days to organize "the take-off."

The CIA continued to fund the MIT Center for International Studies, following *Dynamics of a Soviet Society*—providing $3 million of the centre's $9 million income during its first decade.[30] Rostow would go on to direct a study called *Prospects for Communist China*. Studies by other researchers included understanding the Soviet Union's "slave-labour" system; how communist regimes used psychological techniques to "brainwash" their populations; and how to counter communist influence in developing countries—a topic that was also of interest to the Ford Foundation. The foundation found fame—together with the Rockefeller Foundation—for funding research into the high-yielding crops in Asia and Latin America that gave rise to what is now called the Green Revolution. Though it wasn't completely motivated by pure altruism. We know this because its 1953 annual report states clearly that Ford Foundation's aid was designed to help "those nations whose political philosophy and objectives ... are incompatible with Communism."[31]

The Ford Foundation had come on board as a funder for the MIT center shortly after the CIA, and ended up becoming the its single largest donor, contributing $4 million in the center's first decade. One of its first grants went to a study on economic development in India, Indonesia and Italy, three countries where communist parties were popular, or in power.

A team of MIT economists began meeting with representatives of Indonesia's government. The government was understandably wary of offers of large-scale investment, having just won its freedom from Dutch colonial rule. Jakarta was more interested in technical advice, especially around an idea to develop cooperatives, a model of business ownership where employees are the shareholders, and where large amounts of capital investment are not always a necessity. This did not go down too well with the MIT economic advisers and they did their best to talk the government out of this idea. It may be that they saw cooperatives as a proxy for socialism or, worse, communism. Instead, they recommended that Indonesia needed to allocate two or three times more capital to achieve take-off, according to Rostow's template for growth.[32]

There's some evidence that the Ford Foundation was starting to sense that the MIT group was crossing the line from research into advocacy. Ford's leadership was also concerned at the overlap between research and intelligence gathering, as its representative in Indonesia at the time, John Bresnan, wrote in his memoir *At Home Abroad*.[33] The foundation's suspicions were not misplaced. At around the same time that it had been funding economists, the US government had also, secretly, been arming the Indonesian military, as the writer and journalist Vincent Bevins writes in his carefully researched book *The Jakarta Method*.[34] In 1965 Indonesia's first president Sukarno was overthrown in a military coup backed by the US. Concern over a possible communist takeover was among the triggers for the coup,[35] but it then led to between 500,000 and 1 million people being targeted, picked up by the military or its proxies, and killed. Vincent calls it the largest program of mass-murder in the name of anti-communism since the end of World War II. Indonesia's first multi-party government would be replaced by a military dictatorship, which would rule for the next 30 years.

The Ford Foundation closed its Jakarta office shortly before the coup, and when it reopened the following year, the MIT economists were gone—their place taken by the Harvard Development Advisory Service. Although some of the language of economic advice was to change—there would be no more mention of "take-offs"—the broad thrust of policy advice would be the same: Indonesia was advised to accelerate its capital spending in order to boost growth.

The military government's new economics team was excited about its new Harvard advisers—a number of them had trained at US universities on Ford Foundation scholarships. And, together, they applied a distinctly GDP-centered approach to economic policy. Between 1967 and 1977, investment increased at an average annual rate of 15 percent, just as the MIT team had earlier recommended, and the economy grew at a healthy 8 percent per year during that decade.

But the fruits of this growth were uneven, as economist David Dapice, a member of the Harvard team, reported in the project's official report.[36] After the first decade of military rule, four out of five people working on farms were on less than poverty-level wages. Of more than 4 million non-farming jobs created between 1971 and 1976, five out of six went to self-employed people or unpaid family members. Dapice's data show that the bulk of the growth was concentrated in a small group of industrialists—possibly also members of the armed forces. As Dapice remarked somewhat ruefully: "A minority of the population enjoys quite rapid growth in income while the large majority of the population faces low—and in some cases zero—growth in their levels of living." Indonesia was discovering that growth and inequality seem to go hand-in-hand, just as Pakistan's Mahbub ul Haq had observed a decade earlier. But for the United States, it was largely mission accomplished: Indonesia was firmly within the US orbit, and it had a growing economy to boot.

◆

Stages of Economic Growth fulfilled Walt Whitman Rostow's pledge to his younger self. As a stripling undergraduate at Yale in the 1940s Rostow had vowed to devote his life to combating

Marx and to studying how economies grow—what is described as modernization theory. But Rostow would accomplish far more: he would be an active participant in enabling America's government, the CIA, MIT and Harvard, and funders such as the Ford Foundation, to connect academic economists and their theories to the mission to support military dictatorships in countries that were emerging from centuries of European colonial rule.

Rostow probably had more in common with Marx than he would care to admit. Both wanted a better life for citizens of the poorest countries. Both believed that this could be achieved in stages. And both advocated—or at least understood—that their aims could not be achieved without some degree of violence. In Marx's theoretical case—he never lived to see the Soviet Union—it would be through a revolution of the poor seizing control from the rich. Rostow justified economic modernization through colonization, the CIA's clandestine funding of dictatorships, and the brutality of the Vietnam War—of which he was a relentless and unreconstructed advocate.

While Rostow often advocated that nations must be free to choose their own destinies, in *Stages* he says clearly how traditional societies that discovered modern science did not magically migrate to become modern without violence. Rostow recognized that Britain, France, Germany, the Netherlands, Portugal and the United States needed colonial violence in order to take off and grow. And he believed that non-Western societies may not have developed without it. That, as historians of empire have subsequently shown, is far from accurate. India's GDP, for example, experienced a steep fall at around the same time it became a British colony. For Rostow, forcibly taking over the administration of other countries, changing their laws, levying taxes, confiscating land and property—all were justified as a means to a noble end.

Another paradox for our GDP story is that Rostow the "growth-man"—to borrow a phrase from his Republican sceptics—was no cheerleader for GDP. He understood it was a poor proxy for prosperity, and understood it could be gamed—calling it "the numbers racket" during his Moscow trip. He seemed ambivalent about its application: when fending off his fellow economists' criticisms of his theory, Rostow declared that GDP was an inappropriate measure of a country's take-off; but there's not much evidence that Rostow actively objected to measuring growth through GDP—at least from the records of the MIT Center for International Studies.

If anything, Rostow's predictions for China and India proved remarkably prescient. He wrote in 1959 how both countries were not only ready for take-off, but that they would soon be challenging the established superpowers. "The arena of power will enlarge to become, for the first time in history, truly global," Rostow wrote. "The image of a bi-polar world in which all but Moscow and Washington are spectators, is inaccurate now, and it will become progressively more inaccurate with the passage of time. We are, in effect, approaching an age of diffused power, in which the image of Eurasian hegemony, fearful and enticing, will lose its reality."

Walt Whitman Rostow was, ultimately, an exemplar of the kind of researcher for whom policy influence trumps most other considerations. He felt no compulsion to show his workings, or underlying research data. He had no hesitation, as so many researchers rightly do, in offering an opinion that did not represent the consensus of evidence. David Halberstam notes how Rostow's "firmness in the belief of his own ideas; a lack of healthy scepticism about them; a lack of reflectiveness open-mindedness" grated with Rostow's professional colleagues, as we saw in the Konstanz conference. But it mattered less to Rostow that his findings could not be replicated by his peers; or that lives would be lost as a consequence of his recommendations.

Stages of Economic Growth: A Non-Communist Manifesto is accessible, inviting, and engaging. But it is also dogmatic, and, ultimately, dangerous. Rostow had a black-and-white view of the things he cared about. Once he had made up his mind, that was it; his aim was to persuade you, the reader, to agree and join him on his journey. And the more important you were, the better for him.

Six

The Talented Mr. Strong

*The industrial civilization has promoted
the concept of the efficient man. Groups or
individuals who are less competitive, less efficient,
are regarded as lesser breeds.*
> — Indira Gandhi, keynote address
> to the United Nations Conference
> on the Human Environment (1972)

n June 1962 *The New Yorker*[1] serialized an excerpt from a
book that has yet to be equaled in terms of its impact on ideas
of how we measure economic growth, both in America and

in the rest of the world. The book was Rachel Carson's *Silent Spring*. Such was its reach that President Kennedy ordered his scientific advisers to investigate Carson's claims, and the author was invited to present her findings before Congress. Physically weak from illness, Carson laid out, using the best available evidence at the time, how unregulated use of chemicals such as DDT was harming the nation's wildlife.

And yet *Silent Spring* had not been an easy book to write. Carson was in the late stages of cancer, though she hid this from the public. At the same time she was also subjected to the kinds of personal attacks that today can be found in the outer reaches of social media. Her critics homed in on her gender. They called her an enemy of the state and they impugned communism, the ultimate badge of treachery, as this letter to the editor of *The New Yorker* illustrates: "Miss Rachel Carson's reference to the selfishness of the insecticide manufacturers probably reflects her Communist sympathies, like a lot of writers these days. We can live without birds and animals, but as the current market slump goes, we cannot live without business. As for insects, isn't it just like a woman to be scared to death of a few little bugs! As long as we have the H-bomb everything will be OK."[2]

At least one chemical company threatened her publisher, Houghton Mifflin, with libel, and the National Agricultural and Chemical Association funded a PR campaign. In the words of Robert H. White-Stevens, a professor of biology at Rutgers University, "If man were to follow the teachings of Miss Carson, we would return to the Dark Ages, and the insects and diseases and vermin would once again inherit the Earth."[3]

At the core of their argument, Carson's adversaries claimed that *Silent Spring* had created fear and hysteria about chemicals, which would undermine the many good things that chemicals do. There was undoubtedly some truth to this, but her opponents were not that interested in an argument over the balance of evidence in her claims. *Silent Spring* posed a deeper and more fundamental problem to its critics. Carson was questioning the wisdom of growth based on a lightly regulated if not unchecked industrialization. In doing so she was questioning the very basis of America's economy and of the economies of other rich countries.

That is what made her a voice to be reckoned with, but at the same time it is this aspect of her book that attracted an influential group of followers, including many whom we will meet in this chapter. While Dudley Seers and Mahbub ul Haq were part of a small group of rising stars among GDP-skeptic economists, Rachel Carson would boost the ranks of another, potentially larger group of expert critics of GDP. These would be the environmentalists; they would question the routes through which growth was being achieved, and how we measured it, not so much from the perspective of the poor, but from the point of view of the planet.

◆

A decade after *Silent Spring*, four authors would write or publish their own books questioning how economic growth is promoted and measured. Aurelio Peccei's *The Limits to Growth*, Fritz Schumacher's *Small Is Beautiful*, Herman Daly's *Steady State Economics*, and Maurice Strong's *Only One Earth* spoke to the same broad concerns: that growth as currently constituted carried environmental risks, and that this kind of growth on its own would not end poverty. All would to some degree trace their lineage back to Rachel Carson by drawing attention to the paradox of new technologies. Technologies such as the internal combustion engine, the jet engine, and industrial-scale farming, as well as the revolution in computing, had helped to boost economic growth and improve our lives beyond measure, they would say. At the same time, new technologies were also the cause of environmental problems, some of which were likely to be irreversible.

A fifth writer, Jerome Ravetz, the author of *Scientific Knowledge and Its Social Problems*, had a slightly different message: he warned that science needed a better system of checks and balances as we deepened our ability to discover, invent, and alter the natural world. *Scientific Knowledge and Its Social Problems* drew attention to the lack of quality control in today's scientific enterprise. Even today scientists cannot be censured for professional wrongdoing or for making mistakes in the way that doctors and accountants can.

Arguably the most influential among the readers of *Silent Spring* is Canadian diplomat and businessman Maurice Strong, the founding executive director of the UN Environment Programme, who died on November 28, 2015, at the age of eighty-six. That environmental protection and climate change are now thoroughly mainstream concerns has a lot to do with Strong and his genius at persuading world leaders to create ministries of the environment. Today, every country has such a ministry, but back in 1970 that wasn't the case. It is largely because of Strong that we have a government department in every country whose reason for existing is to challenge and test the claims that new policies can create economic growth, and to test them against globally agreed environmental standards. That is why he is important to our story.

Rarely in the history of environmental policy has a single individual wielded as much influence as Strong. In his prime,

time and again Strong would persuade heads of state and governments to do things that they thought they didn't really want to
do. "Maurice has this ability to reach out and grab world leaders
by the arm, whether they liked it or not," Jonathan Lash, former
president of the World Resources Institute in Washington, DC,
told me in 2009. "He used his access and networks shamelessly
for all of us. Long before iPhones, the net and Twitter, we had
Maurice."[4] In a tribute shortly after his death, Strong's one-time
colleague, the writer John Ralston Saul, said: "What he brought
to the table was not only conviction and organizational skill. He
had a rare talent for bringing together two opposites—highly
original conceptual thinking and highly pragmatic approaches to
getting things done. He was able, for example, to conceptualize
and explain sustainable development when no one knew what
it was."[5]

◆

Maurice Strong was born in 1929 in a rural part of Canada called
Oak Lake and to a family that had fallen on desperate times as
the Great Depression turned rural North America into a dust
bowl. As he would write movingly in his autobiography, *Where
on Earth Are We Going?*, his Depression-era experiences would
never leave him. "The Depression was one of the great shaping
forces in my life, a calamity visited not just on my family but on
my community and my country and on many millions of people
around the globe. Its cruelty stripped my father of his livelihood
and his sense of self worth. It ruined my mother's health and in
the end it killed her.

"Human life, politics, the way society was ordered, had gone
dreadfully wrong, that was clear enough even to me as a child.

But no one seemed to know what to do, or indeed if there was anything that could be done. I used to watch the trainloads of the homeless and the desperate passing by my house, crossing the prairies, torn from their families by need and hunger, and their worn, pinched, anxious faces haunted me for years afterward."[6]

The Depression meant that Strong's father, Frederick Strong, lost his job as a telegraph operator at Oak Lake railway station, and the family was reduced to what Strong acknowledges was "subsistence level"; this is aid-speak for the kind of poverty experienced by only the poorest in the poorest countries. Throughout these years the family lived off irregular food from local farmers and the kindness of a local grocer who would extend credit knowing that the chances of being paid back were slim to nonexistent.

"The long and extreme prairie winters were especially difficult. At times my father had to go out into the bush to cut wood without proper shoes; he'd wrap his feet in rags to keep them warm," Strong wrote. "We moved from one rented house to another, but none had central heating or indoor plumbing. Because we couldn't afford the luxury of coal to keep the stove burning all night, the temperature inside on winter mornings was much the same as outside; our clothes would freeze stiff."[7] At times, the Strongs were reduced to eating weeds and dandelion flowers.

In spite of such painful hardships Maurice Strong says as a child he was happy in his own company and developed a deep love and knowledge of the natural world. He would spend hours and hours outdoors, sometimes skipping lessons to watch the busy, social lives of ants, bees, and the great variety of life in and around his home. His mother, the daughter of a medical doctor and a journalist, encouraged him to read and never tired of her son's constant and perceptive questions. "If nature could be so right," he once asked her, "how could human society be so wrong?" Later, when the economy picked up as unemployed men enlisted to fight in the Second World War, Strong would ask his teachers, "Why does it take a war to produce jobs; [why does it take a war to produce] the resources to get an economy moving?"[8]

Leaving school in 1943, at age fourteen, Strong, too, would join the ranks of young men heading for the front line. In his autobiography he recalls waiting to board a freight train near his home when he spotted a discarded copy of the local newspaper, the *Regina Leader Post*. Strong read that Churchill and Roosevelt had decided that once the war was over they would jointly create a global organization "to ensure that the world would never again have to experience the horrors of war." Strong writes of being transfixed. "I remember the story so clearly. All around me people were going off to the front. People I knew were being killed and tales of human devastation were daily fare. So when Churchill and Roosevelt met and said that the world was going to be a different place afterward, I knew at once that I wanted to be part of that endeavour."

The "global organization" Strong talks of was the United Nations, just an idea in the minds of two world leaders, but born of a desire for lasting peace and prosperity after the Great Depression, the Holocaust, and six tragic and bloody years of world war.

◆

In late 1969, at the age of forty, Strong would eventually realize his childhood ambition, follow in the footsteps of Churchill and Roosevelt, and take on a world-changing UN job. Strong was running Canada's international aid program when he was approached by Swedish diplomat Sverker Åström, who wanted to know if Strong could help the Swedes to pull off one of the most ambitious projects ever conceived in international diplomacy: this was to be the world's largest international conference on the environment, and it was due to take place in Sweden in June 1972.

If there was ever a country in the world that embodied the best of the early postwar, post-imperial European nations, that country has to be Sweden in the 1960s and 1970s under its Social Democratic Party government. As *The Guardian* newspaper columnist Andrew Brown writes in *Fishing in Utopia*, a memoir of his years living in Sweden, "The Social Democrats had inherited a poor, formal and patriarchal society, and turned it into a rich, feminist and fiercely egalitarian one."[9] Much of this transformation was conceived and executed by prime minister Olof Palme, the son of aristocrats, who had a taste for reform—radical reform. As minister of transport, he switched the entire country's drivers to driving on the right.[10] As minister of education in 1968, Palme took part in anti–Vietnam War protests.

Sweden under Palme's premiership was in charge of the upcoming UN conference that would be held in Stockholm. Only this would be no ordinary UN conference (they occur around the world daily). It would be the first ever gathering of world leaders on the topic of protecting the world's environment. The conference was due to take place on June 15 and 16, 1972, and would be attended by senior representatives from UN member states from both the developed and developing countries.

Sweden and the environmental groups that had helped to put it on the agenda saw the meeting as a genuine opportunity to apply some gentle brakes on the growth train. One way to make this happen was for the conference to agree to the creation of a new UN-backed organization charged with protecting the environment. Through such an organization, every nation would get to have an environment ministry. Having an environment ministry also meant having a full-time cabinet-level minister whose sole job was protecting environmental interests. This would be the minister who would ask awkward questions every time any of his or her colleagues wanted to rush through a new chemical factory or nuclear power plant.

Except that the Swedish plan, having gotten this far, had come dangerously close to unraveling. Important progress had been made, such as persuading world leaders and the UN machinery that such a conference had to be held, fixing the date, and finding a venue. But other things were not going according to plan.

United Nations diplomacy in the postwar years was organized differently from how it is today. The then Soviet Union also led a powerful bloc of nations that included much of Eastern Europe up to the Baltic states, as well as Cuba. America and its European allies, led by the UK, were the main counterweight. Countries that chose to remain outside of the US/Soviet sphere included India, China, large parts of the developing world, and Sweden. Arguments were raging over the conference agenda, over who could and couldn't attend, and, perhaps most controversial of all, over the very existence of an environmental threat.

Paradoxically for our story, the countries independent of US/Soviet influence chose as their spokesman for the conference the Pakistani economist Mahbub ul Haq. Haq, as we saw earlier, had left Pakistan shortly after his "twenty families" speech and was deep on his journey from growth-centered economic planner to GDP-skeptic. Ironically enough, however, his new perch was as a senior executive at the World Bank in Washington, DC, the very institution that would force many of the poorest countries down a growth-oriented path through a process called Structural Adjustment.[11]

Though Haq would later go on to co-found the Human Development Index as an alternative to GDP, when it came to environmental protection, he was decidedly old-school and regarded the Stockholm conference as a kind of suicide note for developing nations. Why, asked Haq, should developing countries attend a conference to protect the environment if the result meant having to take longer to industrialize? Worse, why should they attend a conference if the outcome was not being allowed to industrialize at all? It seemed to Haq illogical that any developing country would want to go, and, initially at least, he saw no need to make common cause with environmental groups in his own anti-GDP efforts. "The Third World is not merely worried about the quality of life, it is worried about life itself," he said with barely disguised sarcasm.[12]

It wasn't just developing countries that were angry at being dragooned into going to Stockholm. Many developed countries, too, would not have lost much sleep had the conference failed. This was the time of the Cold War. Germany was still two countries, and America wanted then communist East Germany excluded from the conference on the grounds that East Germany wasn't a "real" country, as it wasn't then a member state of the UN.[13] Naturally, the Soviet Union begged to differ, but as the United States wouldn't budge, the entire communist bloc withdrew.

Having succeeded in getting a global environment conference onto the UN schedule, Sweden had lost control of the agenda. Now with its diplomatic efforts unraveling, this small

Nordic nation with outside liberal ambitions was looking out of its depth.

◆

Sweden wanted Strong to become the conference secretary-general, in effect its organizer in chief, and it is safe to say that Strong didn't need much persuading. "This was an offer I was incapable of resisting," he says in his memoir. The US government turned out to be enthusiastic about the appointment, even offering to host a meeting with Strong. One reason why America might have given Strong the green light so quickly is because the relatively unknown businessman was not expected to succeed where more experienced diplomats had failed. Strong acknowledges that his colleagues in Canada had also warned him not to accept. But, as he says in his book, "If this was intended to warn me off, it had the opposite effect."

And so in January of 1970 Maurice Strong and his family relocated to Geneva, home to the conference secretariat. Priority number one was to improve relations with the Soviet Union and ultimately reverse the communist boycott. Priority number two was to bring the developing countries, an even larger group, back to the table. Priority number three was to create a conference agenda (and conference outcomes) that would somehow steer a middle course between competing interests, while at the same time staying as faithful as possible to Sweden's original goals.

Strong's memoir, *Where on Earth Are We Going?*, apart from being an account of a fascinating life, is also a series of master classes in diplomacy. One of his first acts upon getting to Geneva was to appoint a high-level Soviet official to his conference office. Strong didn't just want any old official, however; he chose one of the country's distinguished scientists. This itself could have caused a minor diplomatic incident, as usually UN civil servants cannot tell governments whom they should or shouldn't appoint to their staff. But after some initial opposition from the Soviet delegation, Strong, not for the first time, got his way. The appointment had two effects: first it meant that the Soviet Union was now formally represented on the conference staff. Second and perhaps more importantly, Strong had engineered for himself a direct line to Moscow. He could now talk to the highest levels in the Soviet Union without anyone else knowing, or getting in the way. With the communist boycott on its way to being partially settled, Strong next turned his attention to another looming crisis.

The developing countries, strongly influenced by Mahbub ul Haq, were taking the line that environmental protection was something that countries did *after* they became rich. They were also angry at the fact that rich countries, those that had damaged the environment, didn't seem to want to pay to clean up the mess they had caused. In the very least, the developing nations wanted the conference to conclude with a cleanup fund that they could draw on, but developed countries were opposed to this, as it would mean admitting liability and could lead to massive legal claims. When Strong saw the draft agenda, he discovered that their concerns had not even been acknowledged, let alone addressed. "Like a skilled lawyer [Haq] hammered home all the reasons why developing countries should not be drawn to participating in the conference on the terms set by the industrialised countries," he recalls.[14]

Strong knew that the conference would collapse unless the developing countries participated, and once again he delivered his trademark diplomatic coup. Strong had sensed correctly that Mahbub ul Haq liked an intellectual challenge, and so, as with the Soviets, he invited the economist onto the conference's preparatory team. Haq, said Strong, should devise a strategy for the conference agenda that would say explicitly that developing countries would protect their environments without compromising their ability to industrialize, and that richer countries should help to finance poorer countries to achieve this goal.[15] And possibly to the surprise of many, Haq agreed.[16]

Co-opting Haq netted one of Strong's more dangerous critics. When it came to the Human Development Index, Haq and his team would famously ignore the environment altogether. But in 1971, Maurice Strong's offer was accepted, and Mahbub ul Haq would become the latest victim to an approach that Strong summarized to me in an interview in 2009 as "never to confront, but to co-opt, never bully but to equivocate, and never to yield."

Within a few months of Strong taking over the conference organization, the mood was lifting and for the first time it seemed that the United Nations Conference on the Human Environment would not be the automatic failure that so many had been predicting. Still, Strong had more work to do. Indeed, there was still one country that had yet to be persuaded and this was the UK.[17] Strong knew that getting UK agreement was critical in part because, along with China, France, the Soviet Union, and the United States, Britain was one of the P5, the five permanent nuclear weapons states which in effect are the UN's most powerful members.

❖

The British government's opposition to the Stockholm conference was partly ideological and partly based on scientific grounds. The government of the day was led by the center-right Conservative Party. Prime Minister Edward Heath wasn't convinced that the time was right to hold such a conference, and Heath's officials had a list of concerns that they wanted answers to. Why weren't all of the world's top scientists agreed that the planet was in peril? What did scientists at the top British universities have to say? Back in 1972 there were far fewer scientists working on environmental problems than is the case today, and there was certainly no consensus on whether or not human activity was affecting the planet in an irreversible way.

Did the UN really need expanding? Did the citizens of the world really need more government involvement in their lives? At the same time UK officials were also concerned that more environmental protection would put a brake on growth. The Heath government published a forty-page color booklet titled *The Human Environment: The British View*, in which it said unequivocally, "Suggestions have been made for a central UN agency for the environment. The United Kingdom is not inclined to support the formation of a new body."[18]

To put it more crudely, what was also happening here was that top officials from the UK, the nation of Keynes and Cambridge, the nation that helped give birth to GDP, were not about to let the representative of one of its former dominions (Canada) set the global agenda. And no one more than Maurice Strong knew this. At the same time, he also understood that his underdog status with the British delegation could also be a strength, especially when it came to building confidence among developing nations and with their spokesman, Mahbub ul Haq. In an interview in London in 2009, Strong shared the secret to straddling these two worlds. "I have always been radical but have always presented my arguments in non-radical terms," he told me. "So I would never use terms such as 'imperialist,'" he said. "I would always present a radical case in a non-radical way."[19]

In the run-up to the conference, London canvassed its top experts and, not unexpectedly, the scientists consulted backed their government's line that it was too soon to take concrete steps. Lord Solly Zuckerman, the government's formidable former chief scientific adviser, who had served under Winston Churchill, said that the environmental threat was not as serious as claimed by Strong and his team. "The prophets of doom," declared Zuckerman, were wrong. The history of the Earth tells us that the planet has great reserves of resilience and can bounce back when threatened—as it has in past times.

"There are some extremists," Zuckerman would say provocatively, "professional scientists not among them, but men who comment from the sidelines, who see pollution as a menace which must inevitably grow. I, however, know of no scientific evidence for this view whereas I know from my own experience that devastation of the landscape can be corrected, that rivers can be cleaned; that skies can be cleared."[20]

Strong could see that the UK would not be easily convinced and decided that he needed to work on parallel tracks. As before, he would try to co-opt Zuckerman and attempt to bring him into the tent. But at the same time Strong knew that in order to get London to take him seriously, he needed more scientific voices on his side of the argument; they had to be credible voices who could counterbalance Zuckerman's. Furthermore, he needed to show the British government that he wouldn't be a pushover, that he had steel.

Strong responded to the charge that his office was little more than a cardboard box of scientific flakes by searching for independent scientists who could confirm that there was a planetary emergency. One way to do this was to appoint his own brain trust, an expert group, respected by his critics in London, who could provide valuable intelligence on what London was thinking and who would ultimately be loyal to Maurice Strong.

Alongside Mahbub ul Haq, Strong enlisted the help of Martin Holdgate, environmental scientist and a former senior civil servant in the UK government. Holdgate brought the added advantage that he had worked closely with Zuckerman. Strong also invited the writer and economist Barbara Ward. A former foreign editor of *The Economist* and adviser to many a world leader, from presidents to popes, the well-connected Ward took the opposite view from Zuckerman: that lightly regulated technology *was* creating a planetary emergency and the world needed to take notice and begin to slow down the rate of economic growth. "I myself grew up at a time of wholesale depression and unemployment," she would later write. "In a sense the whole fabulous market boom of the last 25 years had been designed to give enough stimulus to the economy to prevent any future depressions. But ultimately our planet is a finite system. Ultimately, its resources run out."[21]

Strong asked Ward to consult with leading experts and then compile her findings into a book, *Only One Earth: The Care and Maintenance of a Small Planet.* "Only One Earth" became the conference slogan, and, against UN advice, Strong gave the book to every attending delegate and invited Ward to address the conference. It is easy in hindsight to see where he was going: the delegation from the UK would be forced to listen to one of their own telling them why they were wrong.

Strong also knew that, to counter arguments from powerful countries such as the UK, he didn't only need men and women of influence, but he also had to find more and better scientific evidence, ideally in the form of research. This also had to be from one or more of the leading institutions of the developed world. The Swedes had clearly gambled in calling a major international environmental meeting with so little documented evidence of environmental degradation beyond reports of the London smog and Rachel Carson's *Silent Spring*. In 1972, knowledge on the global environment was a fraction of what it is today. Back then we didn't know that species are being lost at a rate not seen since the last mass extinction. The debate over whether humans cause global warming (then known as "thermal pollution") was far from being settled. The reports of the Intergovernmental Panel on Climate Change, which confirmed a human role in global warming, were still seventeen years away.

◆

As sometimes happens in the lives of risk takers, fortune smiles just when you most need it. In Strong's case, fortune didn't just smile; it presented itself in the shape of Aurelio Peccei (1908-1984), a then little-known executive from the Fiat motor company whose own outsize environmental ambitions were not that far off from those of Maurice Strong.

Peccei, though not a scientist, was the publisher of a report written by an international team of scientists in 1972 that would become an international bestseller. *The Limits to Growth* forecast social and environmental collapse by the year 2100 if the world economy continued on a business-as-usual path. Collapse would happen, the report predicted, if population continued to increase and if countries continued to mine coal, drill oil, produce food, and release atmospheric emissions at current rates. The report also challenged another common assertion at the time (as is still the case today), that new and cleaner technologies would ultimately triumph over older and dirtier ones. Even if this were true, *The Limits to Growth* said, clean technologies would only delay a collapse in the Earth's life-support systems; they wouldn't prevent collapse. The report's hard-hitting message, which came from scientists based at the Massachusetts Institute of Technology, was what Strong was looking for. Strong got in touch with Peccei and the two arranged to meet.

It turned out that Aurelio Peccei and Maurice Strong, though separated by a continent, did have much in common. Peccei, like Strong, was a child of the Great Depression. He had also had to overcome adversity (he was arrested, imprisoned, and tortured for opposing fascism). Peccei's experiences, as was the case with Strong, would lead to a lifelong commitment to multilateralism and an aversion to nationalism. After the war, Peccei, like Strong, would climb the corporate ladder, expanding Fiat into Latin America, helping to create Alitalia airlines, and turning around the Olivetti typewriter company so it was ready for the digital age.

Peccei was restless with corporate life, his son Roberto, a professor of physics at the University of California, Los Angeles, told me in an interview. As a successful executive, Peccei was used to forecasting where problems might occur and then taking steps to solve them. His travels around the world on behalf of Fiat convinced him that humankind was conducting a giant experiment on the planet with unknown consequences, the younger Peccei says. Industrial pollution; extracting coal, gas, and oil; rapid population growth; and intensive farming were all taking place on an unprecedented scale. Peccei was desperate to know where this might take us and desperate that world leaders should take responsibility and prepare for the future.

"Much of my father's thinking on global problems can be traced back to his first book, *The Chasm Ahead*," says his son. "Our planet is facing an increasing set of macro-problems (population growth, resource scarcity, etc.), which nobody is worrying about. Faced with a world confronted by interlinked global problems, his reaction was to start a process of rational planning without being overwhelmed by the scale."[22]

Aurelio Peccei began to give talks whenever the opportunity presented itself, and he would collar anyone of influence prepared to listen. It wouldn't be long before he began to command an audience at the highest levels. One of his talks caught the attention of the White House, which meant that his name started to circulate in Washington's diplomatic circles.

An early partner for Peccei would be Alexander King (1909-2007), a onetime senior UK civil servant and then head of science at the Organization for Economic Cooperation and Development. This was quite a coup, as the OECD is the very agency that had incubated one of the early GDP teams in Cambridge led by Richard Stone. Getting King on board was quite a coup for Peccei. While working for the British government King had been responsible for ramping up supplies of DDT during the Second World War, but he clearly had had a change of heart, just as was the case with Peccei. Others also began to join, and it wouldn't be long before Peccei found himself rubbing shoulders with like minds from the world's power elites. They decided, unwisely perhaps, to call themselves "The Club of Rome," after the city that hosted an inaugural meeting to discuss the problem Peccei had by now adopted as his broader undertaking on economic growth. He called it his project on "The Predicament of Mankind."[23]

The Club of Rome was inaugurated in April 1968, and it was at this point that Peccei faced more or less the same science question that would confront Maurice Strong in the run-up to the Stockholm conference in 1972. Peccei had captured the attention of some extraordinarily influential people, including Dean Rusk, then US secretary of state. Members of the Club of Rome enjoyed the gatherings he would organize and applauded his perceptive questions, but not all were convinced that anything could, or indeed should, be done about the direction of the world economy. Where, after all, they asked, was the scientific evidence? Where was the data to prove that the world was on the road to hell in a handcart?

Like Strong, Peccei also knew he needed more scientific evidence to back up his claim. His son Roberto Peccei says that he probably believed that science and technology had to be reined in, but that he also recognized that advanced nations paid heed to science. Peccei also knew that the state of actual knowledge on his Predicament of Mankind idea was pretty thin. Authoritative, scientific knowledge on global oil and gas reserves, on the long-term impact of carbon in the atmosphere, on the rate of loss of species, or on how many people the Earth can support was unreliable and geographically patchy.

Peccei's tireless networking led him to a group of researchers at the Massachusetts Institute of Technology who were looking to answer just the kinds of questions that Peccei was asking. But rather than painstakingly record data from observation, this group claimed to have found a faster technique, which they said would be just as accurate: it involved the then infant science of computer modeling. The beauty of their work, according to the MIT scientists, was that they didn't need every single environmental data point from every country, covering every sector of the economy. They claimed that they could make decent forecasts on population, or on the state of natural resources, based on relatively small quantities of actual information, which they would feed into their computers, and the computers would then do the rest.

Today, we rely on computing power to forecast trends and make predictions to a degree unimaginable to most in the early 1970s. We have even coined a new term to describe this phenomenon, Big Data. Back in 1972, computers were rare, and only big corporations and rich universities could afford them, which gave anyone working in computers a certain allure. Along with its "growth must slow" message, what made *The Limits to Growth* compelling for both Peccei and Strong was the fact that it had been produced by a multinational team of scientists and economists and that it used the most advanced methods of its day.

◆

Unsurprisingly, a report that claimed humankind was sleepwalking to extinction would not go unchallenged. Indeed, the questions, critiques, and commentary would come from many directions. Because the state of physical knowledge was so thin, many eminent scientists and economists doubted that a computer could accurately forecast environmental collapse.

The critics included Mahbub ul Haq, as well as the science journalist John Maddox, editor of *Nature*. Haq wrote a chapter in *The Poverty Curtain* dismantling many of the arguments in *Limits*. Maddox, meanwhile, wrote an entire book dismantling the entire concept and he called his book *The Doomsday Syndrome*.[24] One British economist was so concerned that he commissioned his own team of experts to refute *The Limits to Growth*. Christopher Freeman (1921–2010), the founding director of the Science Policy Research Unit at the University of Sussex, called his book *Models of Doom*, with the word "doom" in red on the book's spine, for added emphasis. Each of the critics had essentially the same argument: that the model couldn't possibly be so precise when precise data on many of its variables didn't exist. Freeman called the first chapter of *Models of Doom* "Malthus with a Computer," and in it he accused the MIT group of "computer fetishism."

The Sussex team also concurred with Mahbub ul Haq in claiming that the MIT group's recipe of a no-growth or low-growth economy was in effect consigning developing countries to a future of penury, while entrenching the power and privilege of rich Americans and Europeans. Making a bold prediction of their own, they said, based on the historical record, that all previous "end of the world" forecasts had proved to be wrong and that *The Limits to Growth* would go the same way.[25]

In the true spirit of academic debate, Freeman generously offered the *Limits* team right of reply in his book, and in their own strongly worded response to the Sussex critique, the MIT researchers gave as good as they got. They said that, as economists, the Sussex group didn't really understand the new environmental sciences, nor did they get the new science of modeling. The charge of "spurious precision," they said, was a straw man, as no forecast could ever be precise. And far from being a US conspiracy against developing countries, it was the Sussex group, they countered, that represented a Western, Judeo-Christian worldview, a worldview in which man is omnipotent and can do what he likes on Earth. The MIT team, they countered, was closer to pantheistic Eastern traditions that emphasize the interconnectedness of life. "People who share this concept of man, as we do, would also question strongly whether technology and material growth, which seem to have caused many problems, should be looked to as the sources of solution of these same problems in the future."[26]

The Sussex critique to *The Limits to Growth*, though deeply held, articulate, and powerfully argued, did not echo far beyond academia and would have minimal impact on the upcoming Stockholm conference. But there was one UK voice who had the ability to derail Maurice Strong's project. That voice belonged to Lord Solly Zuckerman, former scientific adviser to Winston Churchill. In *The Limits to Growth*, Zuckerman rightly spotted what Peccei and his colleagues were up to. He could see that they needed science to help make the case for a course of action that had already been decided, and he prepared an equally robust critique of his own.

❖

In Maurice Strong, Solly Zuckerman had met his match. In preparing for the conference, Strong had chosen to invite all three—Barbara Ward, Aurelio Peccei, *and* Solly Zuckerman—to address the Stockholm delegates. Ward would open the proceedings, Zuckerman would appear somewhere in the middle, and Aurelio Peccei would get to have the final word.

It is worth reproducing a little of what was said, starting with Barbara Ward, then continuing with Zuckerman and ending with Peccei.

The Stockholm conference, Barbara Ward said, was a moment of incredible excitement, fresh ideas, and new beginnings. She likened it to other civilization-changing epochs such as the founding of the Han dynasty and the Copernican revolution. But she warned that revolutions in science and civilization were never easy.

People had almost literally to turn their minds upside down and discover that the Sun did not go around them. In their passionate resistance to the idea we can see a terrible sense of vertigo. It was as though they hardly knew where they were any more. Such changes shook people to the roots of their being. That is the sort of time we live in now. We too are in one of those times of vertigo. We too live in an epoch in which the solid ground of our preconceived ideas shakes daily under our uncertain feet.[27]

Ward then moved on to what she saw as the conference's three main challenges. First, "the fact that our total natural system could be irretrievably upset by man's activities," which she said was now not in question. Second, that poor countries needed to be helped to become prosperous without having to implement conventional ideas of economic growth, and third, that global environmental priorities needed global environmental cooperation. "We cannot run a functioning planetary society on the totally irresponsible sovereignty of a hundred and twenty different governments. It simply cannot be done."

With half an eye on the skeptical developing nations, Ward said that economic growth based on lightly regulated industrialization had worked in the developed world for reasons that may not necessarily apply elsewhere. "We could lay our hands on the world's vast supply of inexhausted resources," she said. At the same time, "we [in the rich countries] have social instruments of transfer—taxation, welfare, insurance. We do in fact take something from the clever and the rich and the healthy and the strong to give to those in greater need."

If the path to industrialization was to be slowed, Ward accepted that the richer nations had an obligation to provide more assistance to the newly decolonized ones. They would never accept "that they stay poor, while we grow richer." And, in a statement that could never be more true, she said, "I frankly doubt if they will accept a world society which is so hopelessly lopsided. Their patience will blow up in anarchy before the biosphere reaches the point of no return."

After Barbara Ward came Solly Zuckerman. The Stockholm conference, he began, was taking place in an atmosphere of "confused concern," and he started by reminding his audience that the world owed a great deal to science, mentioning achievements including universities, radio and TV, and advances in medicine. "The developed countries may still be short of houses," he said, "but they have more houses and more houses with baths, running water and indoor sanitation. And more and more people now enjoy the new dimension of personal liberty which the motorcar confers." Hunger and poverty persist, he said, but thanks to science this was "not on the scale which the world has known in the past."

Zuckerman then moved on to the main target of his criticism:

> I have referred to a book, *The Limits to Growth*, which has been hailed—mainly by the scientifically uninitiated—as a scientific statement about man's environmental problems. Its authors led themselves through the circuits of a computer to the conclusion that the only way out for mankind is to slow down economic growth abruptly and to change human nature drastically. We have to alter our social and political institutions so that we behave more

sparingly than we do with raw materials and also so that we divide our industrial product more equitably than we do today. If we do not do such things then we shall be digging our graves.

I feel compelled to repeat something I have already said. I do not believe that catastrophic pollution of the planet is among the worst risks that mankind now faces. In Great Britain, pollution is not increasing. In spite of growth in the population and the continuing growth of our economy, our air is becoming purer, our land is becoming more fertile and our rivers are running cleaner. We are far from being alone in this experience.

In a sarcastic echo of the charge of "computer fetishism," Zuckerman added, "The idea that a stationary state of human economy would have to follow a period of economic growth because of a scarcity of resources, population pressure and falling profits is as old as the industrial revolution itself and its formulation certainly required no modern computers. Whatever computers may say about the future, there is nothing in the past which gives any credence whatever to the view that human ingenuity cannot in time circumvent material human difficulties."[28]

The gloves really were off. When it came to his turn to address the audience, Aurelio Peccei, too, dropped any diplomatic pretense for those he labeled die-hard apologists. "Man is a queer [meaning strange] animal—an arrogant, difficult and aggressive one. He stands in a category apart," Peccei said. "The human system is in the grip of a very serious crisis. Our growth syndrome, if not cured, is going to make this crisis worse.

However, there are still people who do not see, or pretend not to see, the mismatch between human growth as it is now and the finite nature of our planet."[29]

Later interviewed by the BBC in Stockholm, a bullish Strong would also drop any public pretence of evenhandedness. Appealing directly to Solly Zuckerman, Maurice Strong said: "The prophets of doom need to be taken seriously; doomsday is a possibility. We are today effecting more change [on Earth] in one generation compared with millions of years of human evolution. An increasing number of very serious-minded scientists have produced evidence that the natural world on which we depend is being destroyed at a rate that is accelerating. I am equally convinced that doomsday is not inevitable."[30]

By the beginning of 1972 things were on balance looking good for Maurice Strong. Co-opting Mahbub ul Haq had helped to ensure that developing nations would end their boycott and there were high hopes that the Soviet bloc would do the same. A combination of some new science from *The Limits to Growth* team and a starring role for Barbara Ward at the conference itself was helping to keep the Brits in a corner. But there was still one more hurdle he had to overcome.

◆

The 1972 United Nations Conference on the Human Environment would be a *proper* UN conference, in that it was pitched at the level of heads of state and government. But with the exception of the host country's prime minister, Olof Palme, no other head of state or government appeared to be coming. Strong knew that without at least one heavy hitter, without someone capable of stopping city-center traffic, without a figure large enough to dominate the evening news, the conference's message risked being lost. He needed an A-lister, preferably from a developing country, and he knew where he could find one.

In his final act of "let's co-opt a critic," Strong, not for the first time, boarded a plane to go somewhere his staff didn't want him to go. His destination would be Anand Bhavan, the Delhi home of India's socialist prime minister, Indira Gandhi. UN insiders warned Strong that the formidable Mrs. Gandhi, as the world then knew her, would be the last head of state to attend. She was, after all, from a developing country. Moreover, she didn't have a huge amount of free time. India had just come out of another war with Pakistan, the result of which was the creation of Bangladesh. Gandhi had backed the new country's freedom struggle and found herself not only on the winning side, but also responsible for negotiations to free a hundred thousand Pakistani prisoners of war.

When we spoke in 2009, Strong retained vivid memories of this more memorable of his pre-Stockholm encounters.[31] "She had a habit of falling silent during conversations and said absolutely nothing for 10 or 12 minutes. Now I've lived among the Inuit [of Canada] and they, too, fall silent during conversations although for much longer periods, so this didn't bother me at all. I waited for her reply and when she finally spoke, she said, 'yes.'"

It turned out that Gandhi had little hesitation in going. And, just as Maurice Strong had predicted, her presence at the conference attracted global media attention and made the event more credible in the eyes of developing nations. Thanks to Gandhi, Stockholm was a truly global affair. When she addressed the conference in her characteristically soft, lilting tones, there was no doubt or ambiguity in her message that humans were guilty of "wanton disregard for the sources of our sustenance." She recalled how her father, India's first prime minister, Jawaharlal Nehru, had objected to the word "conquest" to describe the scaling of Everest in 1953, as he thought it "arrogant" that man should have a "constant need to prove one's superiority."

The environment crisis, Gandhi made clear, was for real, but she was also determined to say that the answer did not lie in less science or less development, as that would be manifestly unjust. What was needed was a different kind of development, more humane, more respectful of different modes of thought and action, and not necessarily on an industrial model.

"The industrial civilization has promoted the concept of the efficient man, he whose entire energies are concentrated on producing more in a given unit of time from a given unit of manpower. Groups or individuals who are less competitive, less efficient, are regarded as lesser breeds—for example the older civilizations, the black and brown peoples, women and certain professions. Obsolescence is built into production, and efficiency is based on the creation of goods which are not really needed and which cannot be disposed of when discarded. What price such efficiency now, and is not recklessness a more appropriate term for such behavior?"[32] she asked conference delegates.

Mrs. Gandhi's intervention is probably an important reason why Strong and not his detractors prevailed at Stockholm. In spite of failing to get the Soviet bloc on board, he had nonetheless delivered 1,200 representatives from 113 countries. He had persuaded them to agree on an agenda that united the interests of rich and poor countries. To the delight of the developing countries, he had outfoxed a skeptical British government and he had made an unlikely environmental champion out of Indira Gandhi.

The 1972 United Nation Conference on the Human Environment ended in practical action: a new UN body would be created to monitor the global environment. It would be based in Nairobi, Kenya, and would be governed by ministers of the environment. As such a minister did not yet exist in most countries, Maurice Strong did not just create a new UN agency; his success ensured that every country would now have a top-level official to make sure that environmental impact would be considered before big industrial policy decisions. Every country would in the future need to appoint a minister to protect the environment.

As we know with the wonderful benefit of hindsight, such a minister would always be in a minority, but he or she would have a seat at the cabinet table and would be able to pose uncomfortable questions to those of his colleagues responsible for delivering growth.

It is probably true that many (perhaps most) world leaders had expected that the forty-two-year-old untried Maurice Strong would become chewed up in the UN's internecine politics. But the man himself never doubted that, come June 15, 1972, there would be a world conference on the human environment, and that he would make it a success.

Seven

"As Vulgar as GDP"

*"Look, you are a sophisticated enough guy to know
that to capture complex reality in one number is
just vulgar, like GDP."*
—Amartya Sen to Mahbub ul Haq (1989)

The 1972 United Nations Conference on the Human Environment would result in the birth of an unusual kind of UN agency. Instead of building schools, promoting peace, or boosting trade, the newly appointed environment ministers in the UN's Environment Programme were there to apply the brakes to the kind of lightly regulated industrialization that has given the world our present style of economic growth. And that would make its existence a precarious one. In his two years as its executive director, Maurice Strong would have to negotiate with many governments that had not wanted the new agency to exist and remained determined that its mandate remain limited.

But the UN's Environment Programme would survive and grow. Two decades after its creation, UNEP and Maurice Strong would help launch a cascade of sister agencies geared to individual aspects of environmental protection and more sustainable growth. The UN Convention on Biological Diversity (headquartered in Montreal) exists to try to slow down the rate of species extinction, which is presently higher than at any time since the last great mass extinction. And it is through the UN Framework Convention on Climate Change (based in Bonn) that countries have agreed to take practical steps to limit emissions of greenhouse gases.

The UN Environment Programme would join a family of institutions that, like many families, is complex, byzantine, and political. I've spent a good deal of the past two decades navigating parts of its organizational chart and I remain in the dark on many things. The UN's main administrative heart is New York, where the secretary-general is based and where all of the representatives of the member countries sit in a grand parliament called the General Assembly. New York is also where the more powerful representatives of the five permanent nuclear weapons states (the United States, Russia, China, France, and the UK) sit in a group called the P5. Nothing of substance gets done in the UN unless a majority of the P5 agree.

Member states on the whole use consensus to decide who gets the top jobs. However, this generous spirit of sharing has its limits. Europe and America, for example, retain the right to choose the leaders of the International Monetary Fund and the World Bank,[1] and America also has a strong say in appointing the head of another UN agency, one of the largest, in fact, which is based in New York: the UN Development Programme, or UNDP, and that is where we go next in the story of GDP.

◆

Whereas Maurice Strong's mission would be to attack conventional ideas on growth on environmental grounds, Mahbub ul Haq would use the discipline of economics to continue on his journey to dethrone how we measure growth using GDP. The Human Development Index, which he helped devise, is the one that has come closest to dethroning GDP. And, as we shall see in this chapter, Haq wouldn't have been able to do it without UNDP, or without its US-appointed Silicon Valley venture capitalist administrator, William H. Draper III.

In 1985, when Ronald Reagan was at the start of his second term as president, Republican Party grandee Bill Draper was preparing to retire from his job as chairman of America's Export-Import Bank and much looking forward to returning home to California and retaking the reins of his venture capital business. And then, as he told me in an interview in May 2013, he received a call from the White House. The president wanted him to take up the job of Administrator at UNDP, in effect the organization's chairman.

"I told the White House that I wanted to go home," he said. "They said: 'Well there's this job that's opened up, which we think you'd be good at,'" he says with a chuckle. "I'd never heard of UNDP, but they said that I would be the No. 2 person at the UN."[2]

Draper wasn't sure what to do, and he phoned a few of his friends for advice. They included then secretary of state George Shultz and the future president and sitting vice president, George H. W. Bush. Bush, Draper reveals, wanted him to stay on in Washington and join his election campaign team in time for the 1988 presidential race. But Draper declined the offer from the elder Bush and accepted the new challenge. He exchanged his outsize Washington, DC, office at the bank for a more modest affair in New York, but one that came with an opportunity to spread freedom and free trade throughout the developing world, which no self-respecting Republican could possibly turn down.

To many UNDP insiders, Draper's appointment was a surprising, if not a shocking, choice to lead UNDP.[3] It shouldn't have been, as the agency had often been led by prominent figures from the US. The White House clearly wanted an Administrator from the private sector to promote enterprise and free markets, in the UN, and across the developing countries. And Draper fit that job description perfectly. That said, Draper, moreover, had some knowledge of how to pull the world's poorest into the middle class. His father, William Draper Jr., was a diplomat and had been involved in implementing the Marshall Plan to rebuild Europe with US aid after World War II.

As he got to know the contours of his new beat, Draper says he knew he needed someone with a radical mind to bring in new ideas. He wanted to shake things up a bit at an agency that Republicans might have looked on, with some justification, as a den of socialists. It is true that many on the left of politics are never happier than when spending public money and often have little or no experience of creating wealth themselves. Draper needed a fellow free trader, an outsider to UN politics, who was available to start straightaway.

◆

In 1988, more than a decade after the Stockholm environment conference and two decades after his "twenty-two families" speech, Mahbub ul Haq was preparing to pack his bags and once more return to the United States. For the previous six years, Haq had been back working in Pakistan, this time as minister for finance in the government of military dictator General Mohammed Zia ul Haq. But his time with Zia had been cut short when Zia was killed in an unexplained air crash on August 17, 1988. With the president were a slew of generals as well as several US diplomats including the American ambassador to Pakistan Arnold Raphel, all of whom died. Mahbub ul Haq was also due to join the party, but pulled out. Richard Jolly, then working for the UN children's fund UNICEF, was with Haq earlier that day and recalls what happened:

"Bill Draper and I were on a mission to several countries, Pakistan, Afghanistan and Iran." They were traveling with Prince Sadruddin Aga Khan and their itinerary included lunch with General Zia and his cabinet including Mahbub ul Haq on the day of the crash. "Mahbub was supposed to join the president afterwards for the flight—but for some reason did not," Jolly says. Later that day the presidential party was returning to Islamabad, having watched a demonstration of the M1 Abrams tank which the Pakistani military was planning to buy. Shortly after take-off their plane started to behave erratically before it nosedived and exploded on impact. "How history might have been different if Mahbub had been on that flight," Jolly says.[4]

There's an interesting paradox in the life of Mahbub ul Haq. Some of his greatest achievements have been made possible by working for Big Men. His first patron in the 1950s was military ruler Field Marshal Ayub Khan. When that era gave way to civilian rule, Haq went to work for another alpha male, Robert McNamara at the World Bank in Washington, and then for General Zia after the military coup in 1977. This ability to do business with strong leaders may well have been partly because Haq was a disrupter, someone to whom bureaucratic processes might not have come easy. His was also the kind of temperament that Bill Draper was looking for in his own mission to disrupt UNDP. Once Haq landed in New York, the two met again, this time in Draper's office. Draper, eighty-seven and a canny spotter of Silicon Valley entrepreneurs, told me he virtually gave Haq a job on the spot.[5]

With his almost fifteen years of Pakistan policy-making experience supplemented by seven years working for Robert McNamara at the World Bank, Mahbub ul Haq knew there was no getting around organizing economies according to any measure other than GDP. And yet he longed for something different and more appropriate as an indicator of economic well-being. As reform of GDP wasn't an option for Haq, he instead pitched to Draper his idea of a new index that ranked countries alongside their GDP but also ranked them according to things that were important but that GDP ignored. Haq was looking for an index that could take into account quality of life, citizens' level of education, and their life expectancy at birth. "Any measure [GDP] that values a gun several hundred times more than a bottle of milk is bound to raise serious questions about its relevance to human progress," he would later write.[6]

Draper says, having heard the concept, he was hooked, though he says what attracted him to this idea was not so much its assault on GDP as its in-built promotion of competitiveness. By constructing a global league table of how countries were performing on the new index, "you could get countries to compete so they [have an incentive to] rise up," he says.

I've tried to picture what Draper and Haq would have made of each other at that first or second meeting. Draper will have been used to being pitched a disruptive idea—it's what happens every minute in Silicon Valley. And at the same time he will have seen in Mahbub ul Haq an entrepreneur capable of fulfilling Draper's mission to shake up a settled bureaucracy, introduce the idea of competitiveness in developing nations, and give UNDP a bigger global profile.

And yet Haq wouldn't come at any price, Draper says. "When I asked him to come and join UNDP," the author of *The Poverty Curtain* told him, "'I can't live on a UN salary.'" Draper says, "When I heard that I said: 'There's gotta be a way to make you live in New York.' So I made him a consultant—consultants are paid per day, so when you add up their fees, it's much larger than my own salary." Draper says Haq was "worth every penny" and that hiring him had been "the best investment I ever made at the United Nations."[7]

◆

So in 1989, at UNDP headquarters in New York, Mahbub ul Haq was back in business under the patronage of a venture capitalist with strong ties to the Reagan White House. He had the title of special adviser to Bill Draper, a small office, a budget, and a guarantee from Draper of total editorial independence. With these conditions met, Haq sought out his old Cambridge pal Amartya Sen.

More than three decades had passed since Sen and Haq had met on their first day as undergraduates while walking toward the same economics class at Cambridge. In the intervening years, Haq's great skill had been in translating and interpreting ideas from academia into practical policy. Sen, on the other hand, had chosen to remain in the university system, becoming a distinguished professor, first at the London School of Economics and then at the universities of Oxford, Cambridge, and Harvard, later winning the Nobel Prize in Economics for his work in understanding how famines are caused.[8]

The two, however, had grown apart in their approach to policy making, so when the call came, Sen, then professor of economics at Harvard, wasn't much impressed with what he was hearing. Sen believed that the UN, with its slow pace of decision making and need to keep everyone on board, would not likely give Haq the freedom to devise an entire new index. He also felt that UN bureaucrats would interfere in Haq's work, and he later told an interviewer, "I kept on telling Mahbub that there is only so much freedom you could have."

Perhaps more critically, Sen was opposed to the Human Development Index's core idea, which was to cram complex and unrelated phenomena into a single index. For Sen, reducing the complexity of human welfare and quality of life to a *single* number amounted to repeating all the mistakes of GDP. "I didn't really want it," he said. "I didn't want one number. I told Mahbub: 'Look, you are a sophisticated enough guy to know that to capture complex reality in one number is just vulgar, like GDP.'"[9]

Sen might have thought the matter finished, but Haq, experienced at getting his way with generals, pressed his case. He understood that GDP's weakness, its relative simplicity, is also its strength, in that it is easy for the nonexpert, for politicians and journalists, to understand. He also knew from his experience of the reaction to his "twenty-two families" speech that lists and league tables of the rich and the powerful can help to generate controversy, what today we would call "buzz."

Haq wouldn't give up, and he continued to woo his old friend. "Amartya, you're quite right," Haq said. "The Human Development Index will be vulgar. I want you to help me to do an index which is just as vulgar as GDP, except that it will stand for better things." The pair continued to talk. "I still remember having really a rather great time," Sen would later say. "He had this favourite Chinese restaurant and we would go there and spend hours chatting away. And something emerged from this." Sen was on board and joined a team of the leading development economists that Haq had assembled, including Meghnad (now Lord) Desai of the London School of Economics, Frances Stewart of the University of Oxford, and later Paul Streeten, who had worked with Haq at the World Bank.

As is the case with GDP, the Human Development Index is a compromise, as well as being an approximation of something more complex. Haq wanted a measure that rewarded countries where citizens' "basic needs" are fulfilled. Sen in addition wanted to reward countries that provided their people with what he called the "capability," or freedom, to be able to make their own development choices. These choices included their desire to live long lives, to learn, to have a comfortable standard of living, to have a satisfying job, to live free from pollution, and to be free to live wherever they chose.

Haq gathered his team for an all-day meeting in New York in September 1989 to iron out differences and find consensus. There was agreement, Stewart told me in an interview in July 2014, on the first two components of a new index, namely, education and life expectancy. However, counting incomes was more controversial. "I was skeptical," she says, and reveals that alternative options that were discussed included inequality and the state of nutrition, which she personally favored.[10] The problem, however, was that in those days data on inequality and nutrition was incomplete or of poor quality. Moreover, she recalls, the formidable Sen was determined to include incomes in the index, as ignoring them would have been too radical a step for mainstream economists and policy makers. He was worried, Stewart says, that without a financial measure, the HDI wouldn't be taken seriously and, worse, that it was likely to be ignored if it didn't.

The team settled on three components for the index:

Life expectancy was chosen as a marker for a long life;
Adult literacy was an indication of the desire to learn;
Per capita income was chosen as a representative number for all of those things that money *can* buy.

With the components in place, the next hurdle to cross was working out a method for calculating the index itself, and here the problem was just as serious as choosing what to include. At least in GDP, each of the variables can be measured in a common currency. Government spending, consumer spending, and business investment are all expressed in currencies such as dollars and so can be added together. But such a calculation isn't possible in the Human Development Index. Adult literacy is measured as a percentage, life expectancy in years, and per capita income is denoted by money. They cannot be added together. Trying to work out the sum total of education and life expectancy is like adding up apples and pears. So what to do? In searching for a solution, Sen hit on the idea of measuring each of the three variables on a scale of 0 to 1. The highest mark for each category is 0, and the lowest that a country can attain is 1.

The index is then calculated by working out an average for the three individual category scores and then subtracting this number from 1. For example, a developed country with high human development, such as Canada, will have a Human Development Index of 0.9. This will be worked out by taking an average score of 0.1 and then subtracting that from 1. Countries with the lowest human development will have an HDI closer to 0.

As the argumentative academics moved slowly toward agreement, their guardian angel Bill Draper was keenly monitoring progress from his corner office. "We would meet every week, sometimes every day. I kept saying to Mahbub, 'Keep it simple. The message has to be clear,'" he told me. As to the message's content, Draper kept to his word. Not only did he not interfere, but he also protected Haq and his team from the interfering reflex of individual governments (especially the US government, parts of which will no doubt have felt that Draper had gone native) but also from the prying eyes of individual UNDP staff keen to know what was in the index, when the project would be launched, and whether they could influence it. "A lot of times decisions get bottled up at the top," he says. "But when you allow decisions lower down, they are usually better."[11]

◆

The spectators didn't need to wait long. The first Human Development Report and Human Development Index were launched in a worldwide media storm the following year, 1990, in May. The opening lines of the 1990 report, partly reproduced here, are a summary of Haq's experiences of the previous three decades:

The use of statistical aggregates to measure national
income and its growth . . . have at times obscured
the fact that the primary objective of development
is to benefit people. There are two reasons for this:
First, national income figures, useful though they
are for many purposes, do not reveal the composition of income or the real beneficiaries. Second,
people often value achievements that do not show
up at all, or not immediately, in . . . growth figures:
better nutrition or health services, greater access to
knowledge, more secure livelihoods, better working
conditions, security against crime and physical
violence, satisfying leisure hours, and a sense of
participating in the economic, cultural and political
activities of their communities. Of course, people
also want higher incomes as one of their options.
But income is not the sum total of human life.[12]

Readers flocked to the report's back pages of statistical
tables, where there were more than a few shocks in store. The
top spot went to Japan, with an HDI of 0.996, followed by
Sweden, Switzerland, the Netherlands, and Canada. These
nations were the world's best in terms of literacy, life expectancy, and income per head. The bottom rung was populated
exclusively by West African states: Mali, Niger, Chad, Burkina
Faso, and Sierra Leone.

The biggest surprise, however, was the United States. American readers of the Human Development Index had to scan lower
down the first page before spotting their nation in nineteenth
place with an HDI score of 0.961. America was tied with Austria,
lower than Spain, Ireland, and Belgium, and only two places

higher than communist East Germany. America's position was attributed to low levels of literacy and life expectancy relative to those of other developed countries. But the shock was amplified by the fact that in 1990 the United States had the world's highest per capita GDP and was expected to be at or near the top of the HDI list too. Haq and his team found themselves in the eye of a storm, but at the same time they couldn't have found a better example of their central thesis: that countries that experience high levels of growth are not the same as those with high levels of quality of life.

Draper, according to some, found himself defending the report from attacks and particularly (though by no means exclusively) from the administration of George H. W. Bush, who had become president in 1988. There was a view in Washington, says Sir Richard Jolly,[13] who later succeeded Haq as HDI principal coordinator, that the index gave credit to countries that had higher levels of public spending, in effect, that it rewarded socialism—Cuba was forty-four places higher on the HDI compared with its GDP ranking.

Jolly recalls a tough conversation between Haq and Draper regarding Cuba's elevated status in which Draper said to Haq: "How could you do this? My friends in Congress will kill me." Haq is reported to have replied: "Bill, your reading of the table is wrong." He then added: "The question is not why is Cuba so far ahead in [human development], but why is it so far behind in GDP." Cuba's lowly GDP ranking, said Haq "shows the price of socialism."[14]

Draper has a different recollection and denies having any pressure put on him from the White House (or elsewhere). What is not in doubt, however, is that the Human Development Report and the Human Development Index were a direct challenge, not only to GDP, but to what is known as the Washington Consensus. We need to remember that the index was launched at a time of deep economic and debt crises, not unlike the time of this writing, except that the countries in the midst of austerity (then known as structural adjustment) were mostly in Africa, Asia, and Latin America. Export earnings were falling and debt was rising as these countries turned to the World Bank and the International Monetary Fund, the two Washington-based international financial institutions, for help. In return, these institutions demanded a reduced role for the state, leading to lower spending on basic needs such as health and education. It is this consensus that the HDI stood against, as the 2010 report, the twentieth edition, makes clear:

> By the early 1990s the Washington Consensus had attained near hegemony, and mainstream development thinking held that the best payoffs would come from hewing to its key tenets of economic liberalization and deregulation. Many Western countries were also reducing the role of the public sector in the economy and lightening regulation. Privatization affected rail and postal services, airlines, banking, and even utility networks. From the outset the *Human Development Report* explicitly challenged this orthodoxy.[15]

While Haq and his team congratulated themselves on a job well done, preparation was well under way for the second and subsequent editions. Haq was not at all precious about how the index had been compiled and was open and encouraging to amendments and innovations. In later years the team would add mean years of schooling to the education index alongside adult literacy. This was partly so that they could differentiate better those countries at the top where literacy levels are 99 percent or higher. More recent reports have tended to include a larger dashboard of indicators, a modification Sen advocated from the earliest years. They also briefly included an index of political freedoms, partly to counter perceptions that the HDI seems to reward some dictatorships.

At the same time, Haq and his team encouraged national and regional human development reports as a way of embedding the concept firmly in national policy making; they also actively helped countries to improve their systems for collecting social data. The first national human development report was produced by Bangladesh in 1992, and since then, more than 700 have been published by practically every UN member state. Among the more popular, with more than a million downloads, were a trio of Arab Human Development Reports that were published beginning in 2003. Written by an expert team from the Arab world, the first of these reports, *Building a Knowledge Society*, highlighted publicly the parlous state of knowledge (literacy, education, scientific research, book publishing) in Arabic-speaking countries compared with countries with similar levels of income. Stung by the very public nature of the criticism, the leaders of several Arabic-speaking nations responded by kicking off a wave of university building and extra spending on research and development.[16]

The impact of the index and the Human Development Reports has exceeded even the most optimistic expectations. In the twenty years since the first Human Development Index, the average global HDI increased to 0.68 in 2010 from 0.57 in 1990. All but 3 of the 135 countries for which HDI is measured have a higher level compared with 1990. Crucially for the project team's thesis, those countries recording the biggest gains in life expectancy and education are *not* necessarily those with the biggest increases in economic growth rates. Meghnad Desai and Richard Jolly both say that few if any members of the project team, with the exception of Haq, anticipated the level of attention the HDI has received; nor could they foresee the effect it would have on countries and how the reports would influence development planning in both good and more questionable ways.

Top Movers in HDI, Health/Education and Economic Growth, 1970–2010

Health/Education	Growth	HDI
1. Oman	China	Oman
2. Nepal	Botswana	China
3. Saudi Arabia	South Korea	Nepal
4. Libya	Hong Kong	Indonesia
5. Algeria	Malaysia	Saudi Arabia
6. Tunisia	Indonesia	Lao PDR
7. Iran	Malta	Tunisia
8. Ethiopia	Vietnam	South Korea
9. South Korea	Mauritius	Algeria
10. Indonesia	India	Morocco

Source: Human Development Report 2010: The Real Wealth of Nations (New York: Palgrave Macmillan/ UNDP, 2010).

Improvements in health/education are measured by the deviation from fit—how well a country does relative to other countries starting from the same point. Improvements in income are measured by the annual percentage growth rate in per capita GDP.

◆

Books and essays have been written about the work of Haq following his untimely death in 1998 at the age of sixty-four. But Haq left no memoir, did not keep a diary, and there is, as far as I am aware, no full-length biography. The few clips from YouTube (courtesy of United Nations TV) are a rare treat for the analyst or historian. According to his friend and colleague Shahid Javed Burki, a former senior executive with the World Bank, Haq seemed to deliberately want to absent himself from history: "Mahbub was not concerned with keeping a record for the way his thinking had developed or was developing. He never saved the papers on which he wrote in neat and elegant longhand. He never filed away the correspondence he received and the replies he sent back."[17]

Mahbub ul Haq did, however, write *Reflections on Human Development*, published shortly before he died. But neither this nor an edited collection of essays published in 2008[18] offers real clues into the reasons for one very crucial aspect of his thought and actions: this is his failure to engage, or lack of interest in engaging, with the policy processes surrounding GDP. If Haq truly wanted to dethrone GDP, then he must have surely known that he would have had to get inside the complex political-cum-statistical world that is how that index is constructed. He would have needed to engage with offices for national statistics and their representatives at the United Nations, just as Richard Stone had done. He would have had to co-opt, build alliances and confront the skeptics, as Maurice Strong had done. But this he never did, or so it would appear. The HDI, for all its successes, had no discernible impact on the dominance of GDP as the world's principal and most sought-after measure of economic well-being.

It is my contention that one reason for this is the reluctance, if not the failure, of Mahbub ul Haq and his team to get under its hood.

Given Haq's open hostility to GDP, relations between his team and the UN team looking after GDP were, not surprisingly, frosty, recalls Richard Jolly. GDP methodology is controlled strictly by an organization called the Statistical Commission of the UN, which oversees how GDP is calculated and gives advice to governments. It is rare for institutions linked to the UN to criticize one another in public, but in 1999 the commission's members took the unusual step of passing a resolution taking HDI to task on technical grounds, which is a polite way of saying "We don't agree with what you are doing, and we think you are wrong." Jolly recalls being informed about the meeting the day before it was due to happen. "I was told they would be discussing the HDI and they wanted me to be present to hear—and reply— to their criticisms." Over time the UN's statistical commission kept its distance "when it became clear that the HDI had so much popular support."[19]

And yet, given the dominance of GDP and the fact that it is embedded deep in the policies of a country's most powerful ministry (finance), reform will never happen without some level of buy-in from the prime ministers and presidents, finance ministers, central bankers, civil servants, and heads of national statistics offices, who collectively keep the faith.

Haq, to my reckoning, made little or no lasting effort to build bridges with these groups. If he did, there's no trace in his written publications or those of his colleagues. Understandably, the established UN Statistical Commission, with its distinguished history going back to Richard Stone and its position of authority, saw the HDI as an upstart competitor and regarded its inventors as a freelance operation.

Not only did he not seek a dialogue with the GDP's guardians, but Haq also appears to have been antagonistic to those environmentalists with whom he shared a common mission (such as those whom we met in the previous chapter). Haq was of the generation of planners and policy makers from developing countries who saw environmentalism as a threat to their ability to prosper, and he took the view that countries need to get richer first, move more people out of extreme poverty, before they can think of spending money to protect "less important" species such as plant and animal life—just as happened in the developed West. Haq once criticized efforts to tackle climate change by saying that "global warming and other 'loud' emergencies are yet to kill anyone." His UNDP colleague Paul Streeten writes that he got into trouble with the green lobby "when Mahbub wanted to say that development means enlarging the choices, not of trees, but of people."[20]

One reason may well be that their argument was not so much with growth as with GDP as a proxy measure for growth, as indicated at the start of the second Human Development Report: "Just as economic growth is necessary for human development, human development is critical to economic growth. This two-way link must be at the heart of any enlightened policy action."[21]

Haq couldn't see this, but the idea that environmental protection is a bit of a Western luxury was going out of fashion even during his own lifetime. Human-induced global warming had been confirmed by some of the world's leading climate scientists by 1996.[22] And the fact that industrialization was directly contributing to the fastest decline in species since the last great mass extinction was also known. There was also a credible body of literature challenging the belief held by Haq and others that countries need to get rich first before they can go green.[23]

Today, top policy makers in countries all over the global South (including Brazil and China) are much more serious about green issues. Yet the old view remains core to the work of the Human Development concept. It is ironic that Haq and his friends criticized the principle that growth automatically leads to improvements in quality of life, but they remained stubborn in their refusal to accept that same critical philosophy when it came to growth and the environment.

Haq was clearly good at building teams, picking the best people, making them want to work for him, and then getting the best out of them. His colleagues say that he was inspirational. He was also used to getting his own way, largely because he chose to work under powerful patrons. They protected his ability to operate without interference and in return he kept his word to them. For Pakistan's generals he delivered on his promise to create economic growth in the nation's early years. For UNDP's Bill Draper he delivered on his promise to create a bold new product that encouraged competitive behavior. He successfully disrupted the UN agency's internal systems and at the same time gave it a much bigger and a global profile.

The approach that both Draper and the generals adopted is well used and well suited to managing creative types. Competent managers who work in media industries and those who work at the top of elite-level sport such as major league baseball or premier league soccer need to be given the right resources and then left alone and trusted to get on with the job. But if Haq really wanted to dethrone GDP, he needed to do more than insist on editorial independence and the right to stand up to powerful nations. Haq needed to bang on doors and build coalitions with groups who might initially not agree with him, which it appears is something he gave insufficient attention to.

To Haq's great credit, HDI remains in vigorous health as a concept and as a set of indicators that all countries now take very seriously. Its annual publication is a firm fixture on the international policy calendar. But Haq's failure to accommodate others in his anti-GDP tent, and his premature death, probably set back his bigger cause. Environmentalists and more green-minded economists, as we shall see, remain determined to supplant GDP on the grounds that continuous economic growth is a recipe for continuous environmental degradation. It is to our collective loss that Mahbub ul Haq, a man with prophetic vision, dizzying analytical ability, and magnetic leadership qualities, was unable to see this and felt unable to work with them to realize their joint dream.

Eight

Exporting Shangri-La

> By now, I've learned that the ingredients
> for happiness are simple: giving, loving, and
> contentment for who you are.
> —Lisa Napoli, *Radio Shangri-La: What I
> Discovered on My Accidental Journey to the
> Happiest Kingdom on Earth* (2012)

n 1971, Bhutan's crown prince Jigme Singye Wangchuck ascended the throne following the sudden and untimely death of his father from a heart attack. The new king was just sixteen. In a larger nation, or in a more mature monarchy, the idea that a young person, not yet out of high school, could take on the responsibilities of head of state would be unthinkable. But Bhutan's new king was wise beyond his years. Already experienced in aspects of statecraft, he was more than ready to take this small, landlocked picture-postcard nation out of the 19th century and into the 21st.

Whereas Mahbub ul Haq needed a decade's worth of experience as an economic planner to see the problems inherent in GDP-centric development, the fourth king Wangchuck would not need nearly as much time. He would, moreover, have the vision to connect Haq's concerns with Maurice Strong's environmentalism—something neither man had managed to do. The teenage king would be the first head of state to attempt a synthesis between greenery and growth, and between growth and well-being. The idea that he would champion has come to be called Gross National Happiness.

"Our country's policy," he said shortly after being crowned king, "is to consolidate our sovereignty, to achieve economic self-reliance, prosperity and happiness for our people." In a speech to mark Bhutan's membership in the United Nations, the king uttered the now-famous words: "Gross National Happiness is more important than Gross National Product."[1]

In the intervening four decades, Bhutan has tried to show the world that it should be possible for a relatively poor nation to become prosperous without sacrificing important elements of its culture and lifestyle; that it should be possible for a nation to grow while remaining green; but that doing so means steering a course that is not only about maximizing GDP.

The king's speech, the subsequent policies of his government, and the work of Bhutanese intellectuals in framing and shaping Gross National Happiness have influenced many heads of government and also major international organizations such as the World Bank and the OECD.[2] At the same time, it has attracted legions of visitors to the nation. Tourists, researchers, seekers of spiritual nourishment, and policy makers have all flocked to Bhutan. They have combed towns and villages and conducted thousands of interviews in search of the elixir, which they hope to bottle and take back home. Search on the Internet, on online book-selling websites and you will see the fruits of their efforts in titles such as *A Splendid Isolation: Lessons on Happiness from the Kingdom of Bhutan* (Madeline Drexler); and *Radio Shangri-La: What I Discovered on My Accidental Journey to the Happiest Kingdom on Earth* (Lisa Napoli). Thanks largely to one king's speech, one of the world's poorest countries has also become the world's laboratory for how to be happy.

This chapter tells the story of Gross National Happiness as perhaps the second-closest alternative to GDP after the Human Development Index. It is at heart the story of a small nation's desire to be able to develop according to its own pace and priorities and to create its own metric, its own measurement, so that it can run its economy and society according to its own values and priorities.

◆

Bhutan is without a sliver of doubt a country whose natural beauty has an arresting, stunning quality. Surrounded by mountains, lakes, rivers, and waterfalls, the country has some of the world's strictest planning rules, designed to protect plant and animal life from being built over. Some 70 percent of Bhutan is covered by forest, and some 50 percent of its land area is not allowed to be developed. There are 677 glaciers and 2,674 glacial lakes.[3] At the end of 2012, the ecological economist Robert Costanza (whom we will meet properly in Chapter 9) was asked by the government to estimate the dollar value of Bhutan's biodiversity and ecosystem services. His estimate came to more than $15 billion, or five times the nation's GDP.[4]

Bhutan, one of the world's smallest nations, with a population of some 750,000, is sandwiched between two giants, India and China. Geopolitics being what they are, Bhutan's leaders have opted for a close relationship with India. India is Bhutan's largest trading partner by a wide margin, and Bhutanese citizens can use the Indian rupee, alongside their own ngultrum, as currency in their shops.

Bhutan until the end of the 20th century was a very poor and largely agricultural society. Most of its people lived on small farms. They grew just enough to feed themselves, with perhaps a little more left to sell at the local markets. Most families did not have electricity, and that meant the working day began shortly before dawn and ended at sunset. No electricity meant no TV, certainly no Internet, and no laptops. Indeed, there were few paved roads and no traffic lights.

But in many other respects, Bhutan belies the stereotype of a nation wedded to tradition. In her memoir, *Treasures of the Thunder Dragon*, the present queen mother, Ashi Dorji Wangchuck, describes her "tomboy" childhood spent gathering wood, fetching water, and harvesting plants. Her father, along with most men, would stitch clothes and shoes for the family, "and of course he was skilled at delivering babies," a practice she says continues in some more remote villages.[5]

Bhutan today is at the center of cyclonic change. It is a parliamentary democracy. It has a noisy and argumentative media.

Centuries-old traditions, the strong families, and confident belief systems are being questioned. But in 1972, when King Wangchuck set out to realize his vision, Bhutan was different. One thing we now know (or at least it is claimed) is that Bhutan's people were among the most contented. Certainly they were among the most communitarian. There was deep respect for parents and the elderly. In terms of rights, faith, family, community, and society counted for more than what individuals might or might not have desired.

Herein lay the dilemma for the young king. Life expectancy was less than forty, and average income was around $50 *per year*. He had decided his nation needed economic development, education, and better health care. More than that, he pledged to modernize governance, including introducing democracy. But he couldn't countenance development at any cost. The king did not want his nation to prosper at the cost of its surroundings, or at the cost of the values its people live by. The king wanted his nation to modernize, but he didn't want modernization at any price.

◆

As a teenager King Wangchuck had been given some responsibilities by his father. He knew that part of the solution to Bhutan's problems lay in better government. By better government we are not talking here about Big Government, of the kind that makes headlines in Washington, DC, or London. Better government for Bhutan meant creating parliamentary democracy in the first instance, followed by a commitment to the most basic functions so that the state can reasonably protect its most vulnerable citizens, especially children and the elderly. As late as 1960 the Bhutanese state did not even have a functioning capital—Thimphu was just an amalgam of villages. And so in 1998, King Wangchuck voluntarily gave up his powers to a council of ministers. A new constitution followed three years later, in 2001. In 2006 the king abdicated in favor of his son, and two years after that, in 2008, Bhutan saw its first ever elections.

Better government for King Wangchuck also meant that health care would be free for all citizens. In the year 2012–2013, a little over 7 percent of the nation's public spending went to health care,[6] which is closer to the average for developed countries than to that for developing nations. Even today, Bhutan is basically a Big Pharma–free zone. There are no multinational pharmaceutical companies: the state picks up the bill if anyone has the misfortune to fall ill.

The results of this policy do look pretty impressive, even if Bhutan was starting from a low base. Bhutan's men and women now live to around seventy years, as incidences of preventable deaths keep falling. The number of women who die during or after childbirth has dropped from 380 per 100,000 births in the 1980s to around 250. Infant mortality has also fallen, from 120 per 1,000 live births in the 1980s to 40 in 2005. These are the kinds of figures you'll more likely see in middle-income countries such as Brazil or Russia. Bhutan, moreover, has all but eliminated leprosy, as well as iodine-deficiency disorder. The vast majority of children are immunized (including in hard-to-reach rural areas), and cases of malaria have fallen drastically, from 12,000 in 1999 to around 1,000 today.[7]

Overall, the health of Bhutan's citizens is in better shape than that of the citizens in countries at a similar level of development when measured according to GDP. Just as nearby Pakistan chose to adopt a development model of private sector–led growth first, with spending on health and education later, Bhutan seems to have fallen for Sweden under Olof Palme.

The king's other big idea was to encourage the nation's intellectuals to think of creative ways to create economic growth, but with Bhutanese characteristics. In particular he was of course looking for ideas that would give practical form and shape to Gross National Happiness. Fortunately for the king, an intellectual with such creative ideas did emerge, though, like so many of the characters in our story, he was not entirely homegrown.

◆

In the late 1980s, Dasho Karma Ura was returning to Bhutan after a period away studying in the UK at the universities of Oxford and Edinburgh, where he read philosophy of economics. On his return, Dasho (a civilian honor the king bestows) Karma Ura established the Centre for Bhutan Studies, a think tank based in Thimphu. A short while later he gathered a small team of researchers from around the world, and together they attempted to give precision to the king's vision for Gross National Happiness.

Dasho Karma is a genial man with a dry sense of humor and a mischievous laugh. In an interview in 2014 he told me that Gross National Happiness is an attempt to quantify what the fourth King Wangchuck had tried to envision all those years ago: "That certain things should not be given up even if they may not make money. We need to preserve those things that are directly counter to making money and therefore to boosting GDP." In contrast to GDP, Gross National Happiness would measure those things that are important to Bhutan's people, including self-reliance, a green environment, health, and literacy. It would also be firmly rooted in its country's cultural story. It would be a way to organize economy and society, just as GDP is.[8]

Gross National Happiness, in the words of Dasho Karma, amounts to an "offensive" against GDP. How Gross National Happiness offends GDP is in its status as official filter for many (but not all) economic development projects—projects that in many countries would go ahead if they were good for GDP. In Bhutan, however, they have to pass the Gross National Happiness test.

Since the late 1980s, most of Bhutan's ministries have been measuring their activity according to GNH, alongside GDP. When important policy questions are being decided, government departments have to ask what impact their decisions will have, not only on growth, but also on the components of GNH. The Gross National Happiness test is compiled from answers to nine questions: for example, how will a particular activity affect psychological well-being, work-life balance, and the number and strength of relationships? If a development project is to go ahead, it should not negatively impact on these, nor must it impact negatively on people's health, education, or physical environment. If it might, then it needs to be rethought.

❖

One of the consequences of applying a GNH filter to economic decisions is that Bhutan has so far decided to stay out of the World Trade Organization.

The WTO is the world's largest club for free trade. Membership allows businesses in one member country to do business with anyone in another member country without barriers or obstacles. It is popular with 161 countries, all freely trading with one another, and there are a further 23 waiting to join. The roll call of recent entrants includes the likes of China and Saudi Arabia, but there are benefits for smaller countries, too. WTO membership enables large international companies to come calling. This brings new jobs and potentially more in taxation and can be good for a country's GDP. But it also brings new kinds of problems that need solving, problems that Bhutan has decided it doesn't need, at least not yet, including fears that WTO membership would reflect badly on Gross National Happiness.

One of the problems inherent in WTO membership is that it isn't always conducive to very small businesses and those that need some protection to help them grow. Senior officials in Bhutan's government know that a large influx of foreign investment can be detrimental for tiny family farms as well as those businesses that have ambitions to become the Fords and Microsofts of tomorrow. And that is because big international companies have a tendency to use their size and scale to attempt to defeat any competition. WTO is the perfect venue for that to happen.

WTO is a bit like a giant open-air market, but one where there are no limits on the size of the shops. A town or village market, for example, will have restrictions on the shape of the stalls. It will have rules on the kinds of businesses allowed and what can and cannot be sold. WTO membership for very small countries, on the other hand, would be like the organizers of a weekly village food market allowing Walmart or Tesco to set up in their midst. The WTO does of course have a dispute-resolution process, but imagine a village smallholder challenging a multinational. According to Tashi Wangyal, an economist and member of Bhutan's national council, although the WTO is meant to level the playing field so that everyone in the market plays by the same rules, "The playing field is not level to begin with."[9]

Bhutan's policy makers also know one other thing that many tend to forget when the corporations come calling: that the majority of the world's older multinational businesses were created and were given the space to prosper in a pre-WTO world. They could grow, develop new products, and find new markets in their own countries and regions without the risk of being taken over, and without the threat of being undercut. In the words of one Bhutanese blogger: "I would rather be a small fire that warms our home, than a big one that burns our house."

The primacy of GNH didn't just stop Bhutan from walking through the doors of the WTO before it was ready to do so; it may even have swept Bhutan's first elected government from power in the 2013 general elections. This was a government that learned the hard way just how attached its people are to Gross National Happiness, and how relatively less attached they are to more conventional ways of achieving economic growth.

Just as in the 1950s, when Pakistan sent its brightest to Cambridge and turned to Harvard University for ideas on how to achieve industrial-led growth, by 2008, Bhutan's government seemed to feel that it, too, was missing a trick and needed to find ways to boost industrial development.

The government decided to appoint the global management consultancy McKinsey & Company to advise on what the country needed to do to boost growth. This was not, at least on the face of it, a bad idea. McKinsey's alumni reads like a Who's Who of both the public sector and the corporate world.

Famous names that once drew a McKinsey paycheck include Louisiana governor Bobby Jindal, former chairman of HSBC Stephen Green, and Facebook's chief operating officer, Sheryl Sandberg.

Traditionally, global consulting companies would be focused on helping other businesses make money. But lately consulting houses such as McKinsey have been deployed by governments to help them to cut costs and to transfer more of what governments do to private companies.

McKinsey has acres of experience advising governments on how they can boost growth while shrinking the size of the public sector. The company itself is good at making money too—the last time I looked it was worth $7 billion, or twice the size of Bhutan's GDP. It employs some 17,000 staff, around half of whom are its famously well-paid and well-looked-after consultants—these are the men and women who travel the world, advising companies, governments, and even charities on how we can all do our jobs better.

Arriving in Bhutan in 2009, the McKinsey team spent quite some time getting their own measure of the country and its potential. They correctly recognized that Bhutan is known the world over for happiness. Happiness is, in effect, Bhutan's "brand." The consultants also recognized that thanks in part to the work of Dasho Karma, Gross National Happiness has become Bhutan's most famous export. Not only is it the standard for Bhutan's own policy decisions, but it is also taught in schools and universities all over the world. It is quoted by heads of state and celebrities and is the topic of numerous conferences, lectures, and seminars. It has inspired copycat measures.

It also didn't take McKinsey long to figure out that Bhutan's happiness brand doesn't make the country that much extra money. Other countries probably make more than Bhutan from an idea that Bhutan gave to the world. That, in the company's opinion, was what needed to change.

McKinsey's consultants are also famously data-driven individuals. One of the skills they are taught is to speedily home in on a problem by analyzing a country's numbers and then putting forward proposals for how those numbers can become bigger, or better. Those numbers might be GDP, for example. Or they could be other indexes.

Bhutan might score high on happiness, but there are a couple of indexes where it is languishing near the bottom, which also caught the consultants' attention. One of these is the World Bank's index on ease of doing business. Anyone who wants to start a new business in Bhutan needs to jump through more hoops than a new business owner would in most other countries. Bhutan is also low on the "tourism intensity index," a measure of tourists per head of population. Bhutan, according to McKinsey, has some catching up to do here as well. Successive governments have been very protective—probably overprotective—about who can and who cannot come into their country. Druk Air, the national airline, has just two aircraft, which at the time of McKinsey's analysis flew to only one city, Bangkok. Visitors, moreover, had to budget for an extra $200 a day in taxes on top of all other expenses, meaning that anyone thinking of a trip to Shangri-La needed to be rich, or desperate to go—ideally both.

According to McKinsey, if Bhutan wanted to create new jobs, if it wanted its economy to grow further, Bhutan had to slash the amount of time it took would-be entrepreneurs to set up and register their businesses. And the country's tourism intensity index had to start growing too. Bhutan had to attract more visitors, from 10,000 a year Bhutan needed to attract 100,000 a year, the company said. The target audience: the increasingly stressed-out but moneyed travelers from developed countries. McKinsey's solution included scrapping the $200-a-day tourist tax and advising the government to hurry up and build more yoga retreats and meditation centers, airports, and hotels. Bhutan was missing a massive opportunity to monetize happiness, and McKinsey would help it to realize this ambition.

◆

McKinsey's advice to Bhutan went much further than just tourism. Other departments in Bhutan's government were similarly advised to scale up what they were good at so that new jobs could be created. The education system had to be reformed, McKinsey said. The health care service had to open up to private providers. Farmers would need to grow cash crops, businesses would need quicker and easier access to credit, and red tape would need to be cut. The entire project, dubbed "Accelerating Bhutan's Socio-Economic Development," was monitored via a "Performance Facilitation Unit," and the eventual prize, McKinsey said, would be 10,000 new jobs in tourism, 30,000 in construction, and 10,000 in agriculture. The company even invented a word that I suspect will soon find its way into our leading dictionaries: Bhutan, according to McKinsey, needed "de-bottlenecking."[10]

Bhutan's government did not immediately challenge the suggestions it was getting from McKinsey and instead got on with the task of implementing the plans. It takes a lot of confidence to challenge the world's leading experts in building nations and growing businesses, but many of Bhutan's officials remained uneasy, and many, including the Royal Audit Authority, were positively angry. There was anger at the $9.1 million price tag that the company was charging for its advice—though this would have been small by McKinsey standards. There was also anger at the way the government seemed to have disregarded its own decades-old golden rule, which was to measure each and every policy decision, not just for GDP, but for Gross National Happiness, too. Did 10,000 educated young people in such a small country need to be working as tour guides, travel agents, and hotel receptionists? If new airports were to be built, had anyone worked out the increase in carbon emissions and what impact this and the extra flights would have on already threatened Himalayan birdlife? Such basic questions needing elementary economic and environmental analysis were never asked, as the Performance Facilitation Unit prepared to monitor progress toward its targets. The only engagement with environment and quality of life was to find ways to monetize it.

Fortunately, GNH is so completely embedded in Bhutan's policy apparatus that many of McKinsey's ideas never saw the light of day and the project is now a part of the country's history. Neither McKinsey nor the government specified a strict timetable for when the targets for new jobs would need to be met, which allowed both sides to save face to some extent as the project fizzled out. Even though the government was meant to be helping the company implement its recommendations, and monitoring them through the Performance Facilitation Unit, officials understood that what was being proposed could impact negatively on the country's unique culture. As a result, some of the targets were either lowered or postponed to implement later. A few were abandoned altogether.

Bhutan's opposition party and the press, on the other hand, had other ideas. They ensured that the McKinsey project would become a big issue when the second general elections were held, in 2012, and it was among the reasons why the incumbent party lost and a new government was voted in.

Bhutan's tradition of Gross National Happiness had effectively stopped it from going down the well-traveled path of economic growth at all costs. Had the McKinsey prescription been followed, and had Bhutan joined the World Trade Organization, GDP may well have increased at an even faster rate than is the case now. But GNH would have been threatened. And so Bhutan's policy makers stepped back, something that the policy makers of very few countries do.

At the same time, Bhutan's policy makers discovered that they didn't really need McKinsey. Bhutan's national income in 2012 was around $3.5 billion. In 2007 it was around $1.6 billion, which amounts to an economic miracle of sorts. For the past decade, Bhutan's rate of GDP growth has been averaging 7 to 8 percent each year, helping to lift the country into the lower rungs of middle-income nations. The population clearly has more money to spend. In the five years between 2008 and 2012, spending by households doubled to around $645 million. Government spending nearly doubled to $300 million in the same period.[11]

◆

And so to the broader question: Can Gross National Happiness be exported to countries outside the Himalayan kingdom? Is it realistic to think that it could have a place elsewhere? If it is, then is it possible to imagine Gross National Happiness becoming a viable alternative to GDP?

To use the language of accounting, on the plus side Gross National Happiness counts among its fans no less than the former UK prime minister. David Cameron is among many world leaders to enthusiastically endorse government-sponsored happiness surveys. In the forty-four years since King Wangchuck's 1972 speech introducing the world to GNH, the idea to try to measure happiness, or well-being, has become a global industry, and well-being surveys are now routinely carried out by governments, international agencies, and NGOs in both developed and developing countries. One of the reasons for this, as we know, is that GDP fails to capture any aspect of well-being, such as job satisfaction, volunteering, friendships, or other kinds of life satisfaction that do not involve money.

Leaders are keener than ever to take the well-being temperature of their electorates, partly to know whether their policies are having a positive impact on the lives of those who will vote come election time. In the UK, one of the more influential proponents of well-being is Lord Gus O'Donnell, an economist and top civil servant who worked with several prime ministers, including David Cameron. O'Donnell has written, "Very few academics of any discipline would now argue that a country should attempt to maximize GDP." He adds, "The era of GDP being the unique measure is now over, and that is a positive step."[12]

On the minus side, while GNH has undoubtedly had an impact at the highest levels in developed economies, it has done so while its supporters try to ignore or downplay one critical feature in its definition: unlike GDP, GNH is essentially anti-consumerism. And that, in turn, has much to do with Bhutan's cultural context of Buddhism. Madeline Drexler, the editor of *Harvard Public Health* magazine, who has spent time in Bhutan, is convinced that GNH could have emerged only in a society where there is no incentive to consume. "Bhutan was a GNH country before there was GNH," she writes.[13]

One of Buddhism's central beliefs (if not *the* central idea) is the need to tackle suffering. Suffering in Buddhist thought is caused by craving. Buddhists believe that we suffer because we crave things, such as material goods. We might want them, Buddhists say, but do we really need them? If we want to reduce suffering, then what we need to do is learn to control our wants; we must learn to control our cravings.

Siddhārta Gautama, Buddhism's founder, is believed to have outlined an eight-point plan (known more formally as the Eight-fold Path) to controlling our wants. Not entirely by coincidence, some of the items in the eight-point plan can also be found in Dasho Karma's Gross National Happiness checklist. GNH values psychological well-being, the nature of human relation-ships, environment, and work-life balance. Each of these, in some way or other, is connected to Buddhist beliefs about reducing suffering and controlling wants.

I asked Dasho Karma if he agrees, but he told me that Bud-dhism isn't against wealth creation; nor is it anti the enjoyment of wealth. "One Buddhist description of heaven is a bit like a ten-star hotel," he said with a big chuckle. Dasho Karma is concerned that GNH shouldn't be seen as too "Buddhicised," as he calls it. If GNH is to become more of a global export, then its appeal and its attraction have to go beyond one culture or belief system. But at the same time there is no denying that among today's major religions, Buddhism probably has the strongest anticonsumer message. That is one reason perhaps why GNH doesn't include consumer spending in the way that GDP does.

Buddhism's Path to Reducing Suffering

- Understanding, believing, and being committed that Buddhism is the right way
- Speaking, behaving, and earning a living in a way that doesn't harm, mock, or insult others, including the natural world
- Learning how to meditate, concentrate, and contemplate

Still, the Buddhist-inspired idea that happiness ultimately is about reducing suffering, helping others, and keeping our wants and our desires under control is at odds with how happiness is understood (or defined) elsewhere. In the non-Buddhist universe, happiness and consumption are often linked. Even Bhutan has been unable to escape the connection.

In the final analysis, Bhutan's own experience is a salutary reminder why GNH is unlikely to work so long as consumption remains an important goal for economies. Bhutan's myriad policies to promote and measure happiness have undoubtedly had some impact on its growth figures, but, just as is the case with the Human Development Index, ultimately the world is measuring and judging Bhutan, along with everyone else, according to GDP and not according to GNH.

Still, to its credit, small, landlocked Bhutan, arguably one of the world's happiest nations, had the foresight and the courage to try to run its affairs according to a metric that wasn't only GDP. Remarkably, the vision for this idea came, not from some wizened academic or from seasoned policy makers, but from a king who was still at school. The fourth King Wangchuck had the foresight to think differently and to a large extent persuaded many other nations of the merits of his case. He may not have succeeded completely in what he was trying to achieve, but we should all be grateful that he had the insight, the wisdom, and the courage to try.

Nine

$33 Trillion Man

*Chemistry has outgrown alchemy and astronomy
has emerged from astrology.*
　　—Herman Daly on economics's reluctance
　　　to embrace the scientific method (2013)

n 1970, a few years before the great publishing sensation
that was *The Limits to Growth*, one of its lead authors saw an
opinion article in the *New York Times* written by Herman
Daly, a then relatively unknown economist based at Louisiana
State University.[1] In the article, headlined "The Canary Has
Fallen Silent," Daly questioned why economies must continually

grow and what the long-term consequences of growth without limits might be. These were essentially the same questions that the *Limits to Growth* team had been asking, except that Daly felt no need to resort to computer-based projections for an idea that he called steady-state economics. "I didn't use any computer modeling," Daly would tell me in an interview. "For me the idea that there are limits to growth was totally intuitive. It is common sense. The computer model helps to strengthen it, but we don't need math to 'prove' it."[2]

Daly, eighty-five at the time of writing, is important to the story of GDP because he is one of the first academic economists willing to bridge the gulf between Maurice Strong and Mahbub ul Haq. He could combine Maurice Strong's environmentally based critique of growth with Mahbub ul Haq's economic one. Like Haq he could see the dangers of a badly constructed index. At the same time, like Strong, he understood that economists need to learn to think and operate inside physical limits. "Chemistry has outgrown alchemy and astronomy has emerged from astrology," he says. But economists continue to work as if they live in a parallel world to the rest of the scientific community. Such a view, as we shall see, would keep Herman Daly at the periphery of his professional colleagues. But his willingness to stand up and ask awkward questions also meant he would become a magnet for the small but growing movement of scholars who wanted to question models of economic growth but had few other people to turn to.

◆

Herman Daly was born in 1931 in Texas to parents who ran the local hardware store. A child of the Depression and World War

II, he told me that in his case money wasn't so much the problem as education, or the lack of it. "My parents weren't college educated," Daly says. "Dad really felt the lack of an education and was eager that I got one."[3] It was Daly's good fortune that Rice University was on his parents' doorstep, and he took his undergraduate degree there before moving to Vanderbilt for a PhD in development economics.

Daly was interested in learning about how poor countries can become richer. He went to Brazil, where he taught and did some research. It was here that he came across *Principles of Political Economy* by John Stuart Mill (1806–1873). Mill was an English philosopher, Liberal Member of the British Parliament, and advocate of human rights, including, as it happens, the right for people to be happy. These days Mill is remembered for being an early supporter of free markets, but Daly also discovered that Mill was no fan of constantly expanding economies. On the contrary, Mill argued that the logical conclusion of growth would be environmental destruction and reduced quality of life (less happiness). Mill concluded that a "stationary state" was surely better.

Daly took Mill's stationary state, rephrased it for the 20th century, and published his signature book, *Toward a Steady-State Economy*, in May 1973. The purpose of societies shouldn't be just to grow, meaning to become materially richer, Daly would argue. Instead, governments should find ways for their citizens to develop in other ways. People should be encouraged to be happy without the need to drill holes in the ground for oil, without encouraging citizens to spend money they don't have or buy consumer goods they don't need.

Like Aurelio Peccei, however, Herman Daly also found that it wasn't easy to convince the people who mattered. In his case, heads of economics departments, writers of textbooks, and even young up-and-coming academics were skeptical if not a little afraid of what they were hearing. That is understandable to a large extent. By the 1970s economics was just about getting used to speaking the language of one new discipline—it was getting more mathematical. Now here was Daly telling colleagues they should forget that and start worrying about physics and biology.

Over the years Daly says that he began to see a drop in students wanting to study with him for their PhDs, not because they didn't want to, but because they knew they'd fail to get past a committee of more orthodox economists in order to receive the qualification. "That any student wanted to do a PhD with me made them prima facie incompetent" in the eyes of other economists, Daly recalls. Just as with the team that put together *The Limits to Growth*, Herman Daly would discover that the world isn't kind to heterodox thinkers, especially those who like to question the views of powerful people. It didn't matter that Daly was merely popularizing an idea from the great John Stuart Mill. What mattered was his skepticism around the need for constantly rising economic growth.

❖

Not everyone who knocked on Herman Daly's door left disappointed, however. One day Robert Costanza, already a PhD, joined Herman Daly at Louisiana State University. Today, of the some 2,000 or more researchers worldwide who study how economics interacts with the natural world, Robert Costanza is arguably the best known to a mainstream audience, if not the most influential. His research has been cited more than 3,000 times, the most for anyone in the field. He has also published with more than 100 fellow scientists, again, more than anyone else in the field to date.[4]

With the mainstream economics profession skeptical of the idea that economics should operate inside the boundaries of science, Daly, Costanza, and other colleagues decided they had to strike out on their own and create a new subfield, which they called ecological economics.[5] Ecological economics is the study of economics that recognizes that societies do not live in an earthly utopia, but on a planet that has constraints, and that economic decisions have environmental consequences.

The difference between a mainstream economist and an ecological economist is often the approach they take to the same question. So, for example, a mainstream economist will want to understand how economies grow; an economist with an interest in public policy (such as Mahbub ul Haq) will want to understand the components of that growth and its implications for the lives and livelihoods of people. An ecological economist, in contrast, will question what growth means for ecology and environment. He or she will not take growth as a given.

One absolutely key question that many (but not all) ecological economists have been asking from the earliest days is what would happen to GDP if the environment were taken into account. Would economies look bigger or smaller if, say, the value of forests and lakes were included inside GDP? And what would happen to growth rates if forests and lakes suffered degradation?

One answer to this question emerged in 1997 in a landmark research paper coauthored by Costanza and twelve colleagues and published in the science journal *Nature*.[6] Costanza and his team estimated that the size of world GDP (at the time) could increase to $33 trillion if it also included estimates for the environment and what is called "natural capital." This figure, along with the team's methods and assumptions, would be fiercely attacked by both economists and environmental groups. Environmental groups especially believed (and many still do) that putting a dollar price on nature is in fact to devalue it. But Costanza was savvy enough to know that without a monetary valuation, and without such a valuation taking place *inside* GDP, environmental protection would continue to struggle to attract the attention of policy makers.

The team was careful to acknowledge uncertainties in many of the figures and as such said that a likely value would fall in the range of $16 trillion to $54 trillion. In contrast, world GDP at the time was $25 trillion and US GDP was just under $7 trillion. It meant that if world GDP included environmental accounts, the total value would be larger than what it was in 1997. Still, one implication of this finding was that many countries rich in natural resources (but poor in other ways) might find themselves higher up the GDP table if environment was accounted for in their GDP figures.

Nature put the paper on its front cover under the headline "Pricing the Planet." As this wasn't meant to be a purely academic exercise, Costanza and his team used the space allotted to them by the journal to ask pointedly why it is that GDP lacks an environmental dimension. Why, for example, does GDP fail to take into account the value that oceans and forests, wetlands and rivers, provide? And why does GDP take environment into account for the wrong reasons?

Costanza and his colleagues wrote:

> What this study makes abundantly clear is that eco-system services provide an important portion of the

total contribution to human welfare on this planet. We must begin to give the natural capital stock that produces these services adequate weight in the decision making process, otherwise current and continued future human welfare may drastically suffer. World GNP would be very different in both magnitude and composition if it adequately incorporated the value of ecosystem services. One practical use of the estimates we have developed is to help modify systems of national accounting to better reflect the value of ecosystem services and natural capital.[7]

The paper proved to be a sensation, dominating global science and environment news coverage for some time after its publication. Partly as a result of the media attention, the paper also generated one of the biggest scholarly controversies of that year.

◆

"Scientifically ill-founded." "Foolhardy." "Flawed." These are a few of the choice reactions that the paper generated from mainstream academic economists, including many of those with a strong interest in valuing the environment. The paper was rightly seen as a direct assault on their field from a scientist most had never heard of, and in a journal that had little if any record of publishing economics papers. Kerry Smith, a professor of environmental economics at Duke University, said in a letter to *Nature* that the paper combined "bad economics with bad ecological science."

For a variety of reasons (many of them good ones), mainstream economists told Costanza that he could do no such thing as put a dollar value on the world's ecosystems services. Among the criticisms, Costanza was told that, according to the "laws" of economics, a free good can't have a price, as it is not traded in the conventional sense: it isn't bought and sold on an open market. Leading mainstream economists also questioned how Costanza intended to go about finding every single piece of environmental service in every country, when in many parts of the world, such data has yet to be collected.

Some of these arguments were the same as those leveled at Aurelio Peccei and his team of computer modelers more than twenty-five years before Costanza's work. The mainstreaming of computers and the advent of Big Data have made no difference: Any number that pretended to represent the value of the Earth's ecological systems, these economists warned Costanza, would at best be meaningless and at worst, dangerous.

Among those economists who would take such a view was no less than Costanza's mentor Herman Daly. In Costanza, Daly had found a fellow academic who could agree that economies must operate inside ecological limits. But Daly could not agree to including the natural world inside GDP and did not join Costanza's effort—though he would not criticize it in public. Daly says that because so much of his own critique of mainstream economics was to question claims of numerical precision, he found it hard to then embrace this when it came to endorsing change in GDP.

Many of the economists' criticisms were justified, and Costanza's team did have some serious thinking to do. How to put a price tag on a forest or on an ocean, when these are hardly, if ever, going to be traded, was (and remains) a valid question. The research team solved this partly by asking what people (or governments, or industry) would want to *pay* if a particular ecological service suddenly ceased to exist. What would a user, for example, be willing to pay if he or she was forced to keep a threatened environmental service from becoming extinct.

A good example of this is the story of New York State's Catskill Mountains. The Catskills provide a valuable water purification service. The water that New Yorkers drink and use for cooking, washing their cars, and hosing their patios comes courtesy of the natural purification system of the Catskill Mountains soils. When it rains, the soils act to purify the water, which finds its way into aquifers before it is diverted into New York City's water supply. If the Catskills' natural aquifers were built over, or if they were allowed to degrade in some way, New Yorkers would be forced to pay much more for their clean water. In 2012, the city authorities worked out that an equivalent water treatment plant would cost $8 to $10 billion to build. In contrast, at the time it cost $1.5 billion to keep the Catskills in good health.[8] For Costanza's purposes, the value of the Catskills would be $1.5 billion because that is what the city's leadership would be willing to pay to keep them in functioning health.

Still, not every natural water treatment system is as well-known as New York's Catskills. For many natural processes, Costanza and his team had to make not much more than an educated guess as to how much someone would be willing to pay to replace it should it vanish (a guess that nonetheless would have been based on the published research literature).

It wasn't just economists who were angry. I also discovered just how opposed some conservationists were to the idea of valuing nature. They thought it vulgar that we should even try to put a dollar price or use words such as "capital" to describe something so precious, so beautiful, and yet so important as nature. Others noted that Costanza and his colleagues seemed to assume that all of nature is worth preserving, when clearly there are some aspects—invasive species, for example—that we wouldn't want to protect. Conservation biologist David Ehrenfeld, quoted in the *New York Times*, said, "I'm afraid that I don't see much hope for a civilization so stupid that it demands a quantitative estimate of the value of its own umbilical cord."[9]

By far the most detailed critique, though, came from the formidable David Pearce, a professor of environmental economics at University College London. A towering figure in his field, he was a sometime adviser to the Thatcher government in Britain and someone (rather like Solly Zuckerman) to whom Conservative officialdom listened. Sadly, he died in 2005 of leukemia at the age of sixty-three.[10]

Pearce, already an established thinker in valuing the environment, had big problems with the $33 trillion figure, which he thought to be massively inflated. Pearce also questioned whether it could ever be possible to know, with any accuracy, how much someone would be willing to pay for each and every environmental service in the entire world. In a separately published four-page review in *Environment* magazine, Pearce called Costanza's work "a violation of basic economic principles."[11]

To illustrate what he meant by this, Pearce used a method of arguing beloved of courtroom lawyers: take one or two facts from the opposing side's case and then slowly but publicly tear them to shreds as an illustration of a larger point. The "fact" that Pearce chose to dissect was Costanza's estimate that the world's oceans have what Costanza called a "cultural value" of $2.5 trillion; or $76 per hectare.

Costanza and his team defined cultural value as what we're "willing to pay" to preserve oceans for cultural reasons. We might like to preserve oceans for cultural reasons because we like to windsurf, for example, or because we want to live in a beachfront house and marvel at the open sea. Costanza and his team did not calculate the $76-per-hectare figure by asking the entirety of the global population what we would pay to preserve the cultural value of oceans. Instead, they did the next best thing, which was to see if such a figure exists in the research literature. Fortunately for them, it did, which meant that the figure could be relied upon, if not as the last word on the subject, then at least as a first-order estimate.[12]

Pearce, though, was skeptical. It is possible that a wealthy person living in a rich country might be prepared to pay $76 for the right to windsurf on a hectare of ocean. Alternatively, a poor person living in a poor country might just be willing to pay $76 to preserve a hectare of ocean if jobs depended on it. But the data isn't clear. We don't really know, because most of the world's 7 billion people haven't been asked.

Pearce said it was illogical to produce a value for the whole world, just by multiplying $76 by the total surface area of oceans (36 billion hectares). It might be possible to calculate a value for an individual area such as the Gulf of Mexico, or Dubai Creek, or Lewes on the English south coast. But it is unlikely that inhabitants of each of these places will all be willing to pay $76 per hectare. Some might be willing to pay more. Others would pay less. Simply taking one number ($76 per hectare), pretending it represents every part of the world, and then adding it up lots and lots and lots of times produces meaningless results and is plain wrong, according to Pearce. "If the oceans were to vanish completely, does anyone imagine that $2.5 trillion would compensate people for the cultural value they would lose?" he asked.[13]

There was one other issue that agitated the mainstream economists even more than a potentially ropy statistic. Economists define GDP as the sum total of output, or expenditure. That implies, to an economist at least, that GDP cannot be exceeded. The logic behind this argument is as follows.

Suppose that my total wealth is $1,000. I cannot then turn around and say, "Oh, and by the way: I'm also worth $1,500." That would be illogical to a mainstream economist, and there is a kind of internal logic to the argument. If I'm worth $1,000, then I cannot simultaneously be worth $1,500. By the same analogy, if global GDP in 1997 was $18 trillion, then it couldn't also be $33 trillion. Even if environmental services were factored into the total, world GDP would still be $18 trillion. What the economists were also implying (though not saying openly) is that environmental services were very likely a tiny, tiny fraction of what Costanza and his team were claiming.

Robert Costanza was angry when I put these concerns to him in an interview.[14] All of GDP, he pointed out, is worked out in exactly the same way. National statistics offices take a sample value for, say, business investment or consumer spending and then use this sample to calculate a national figure for the whole economy. GDP is not calculated by counting every single trade or every single monetary transaction. The technology today probably does exist to be able to record every such transaction, but GDP doesn't use it; GDP relies on sampling methods. "One can of course argue that all macroeconomic accounting is flawed in this respect," Costanza says.

Especially irritating, however, were the claims about inaccuracies in valuation methodology. Costanza points out that ecological economists also have major problems with the idea of valuing an environmental service on the basis of what we would be willing to pay to keep it. But he says his team used it because it is the system that most existing research relies upon. "We cannot be faulted for violating 'basic economic principles' by following the standard practice."

Costanza is also frustrated at Pearce and others' claim that GDP cannot be exceeded. For Costanza, the whole point of valuing nature is to show *precisely* that GDP undervalues a nation's true wealth and that it is incomplete as an indicator by ignoring natural capital and ecosystem services. In a response published alongside Pearce's *Environment* magazine review, Costanza wrote, "Unlike Professor Pearce we do not believe that there is any one right way to value ecosystem services. But there is a wrong way, and that is not to do it at all." [15] Though it is fair to say that Pearce ended his review by saying that although he thought the work of Costanza and his coauthors to be "deeply flawed," its intention was correct: "To show all of us just how valuable the natural world is. That clearly touches a chord with the many people who care about what is happening to the planet."

Although this dispute may appear to be an argument on the technicalities of valuing nature, at its heart it was about something a good deal bigger. This was a battle over the right to set the rules for how economies are to be valued. Mainstream economists, even those with an interest in the environment such as David Pearce, are the guardians of their discipline, its rules and its traditions. The newer group of ecological economists had violated the rules of the group to which they wanted to belong and had to be shown their place. They call themselves economists, David Pearce seemed to be saying, yet they show disloyalty to its intellectual traditions.

Robert Costanza and his colleagues in ecological economics aren't necessarily wrong, though somewhat naively they thought that sticking to the same operating principles as mainstream economists would make their conclusions more acceptable to the doubters. Instead, they found themselves at the mercy of the kind of rhetorical attacks that influential academic social scientists are practiced at. It's a class act that attacks you for not adhering to a higher standard than that used by everyone else in the industry.

◆

In spite of the controversies—indeed, perhaps because of them—the *Nature* paper put ecological economics and Robert Costanza in a leading position to influence the debate about the problems with GDP and how to solve them. However, publication in *Nature* could very easily not have happened. In fact, Costanza and his team were lucky that things didn't turn out differently.

Scientific research papers that appear in the top journals, such as the *Lancet*, *Science*, and *Nature*, need to fulfill a number of conditions. First off, the discovery or invention being claimed has to be original. Next, it must be something that is significant for the widest possible audience of scholars and not just technical experts; and last but not least, the work has to be technically sound, meaning there must be no errors in the calculations.

In scientific publishing there's an extra unwritten convention, a sort of code of practice that anyone who publishes in the top journals is meant to know. Editors at the leading journals compete for the best ideas and the top talent just like elite sports teams. That means if you've submitted your manuscript to, say, *Nature*, then you cannot, under any circumstances, ever, ever send it to *Nature*'s great rival, *Science*.

Only it seems that no one told Costanza.

The previous year, in 1996, the Costanza team chose initially to send their $33 trillion estimate, not to *Nature*, but to its Washington, DC-based rival, *Science*. And unbeknownst to *Nature*, *Science* rejected it for publication. Had *Nature*'s editors known, they, too, would almost certainly have turned the paper down and it would likely have ended up in a more specialized or lower-tier journal. The global media fanfare and ensuing scholarly debate would have been less, and the paper's longer-term impact much diminished.

So what happened?

Approaching *Science* before *Nature* made sense for Costanza. At the time he was based at the University of Maryland. The journal had earlier sent a reporter to cover a scientific meeting that Costanza had helped to organize in the buildup to the big paper. So when the final draft manuscript landed on their desks, *Science*'s editors would have had a good inkling of what was to come and that it would meet their criteria. The $33 trillion finding was certainly original; it was also saying something of interest to more than just economists and environmental scientists. The only question that the editors weren't sure about was the technical one: Was the paper technically sound? And it was on that question that events took a different turn.

Manuscript in hand, *Science*'s editors quickly moved on to the next step, which is to send the text out for peer review— sending it to other experts in the field, who would judge the research for originality, wide interest, and technical merit. Sensibly for a paper that covered more than one discipline, the editors chose both economists *and* ecologists as reviewers. They would have been expecting some criticism for a text claiming to be a world's first. But they couldn't possibly have expected what was to come.

One reviewer, likely an economist (reviewers are by convention anonymous) questioned the whole point of monetary estimates for nature. "Can I purchase [them] and do as I like with them?" he asked sarcastically. He added, "There are perhaps two immediate reactions: foolhardy or brave. Unfortunately, I believe the former is more appropriate. Overall, I believe this paper is interesting as an example of notable individuals feeling they must take the monetary valuation approach to such extremes but is scientifically ill-founded."

Another reviewer said, "Setting aside the issue of whether this is a useful approach, the undertaking suffers in several ways: false precision . . . severe methodological problems . . . and general lack of rigour and intellectual value lends the effort an air of unreality."

Rocked by the severity of the criticisms, *Science*'s editors, embarrassed, felt that they had no choice but to reject the paper, offering no right to appeal.[16] Costanza wasn't one for giving up, though. Weeks after *Science*'s faxed rejection, a revised manuscript landed on the desk of an editor at *Nature*'s offices in central London, overlooking the Grand Union Canal. As with *Science*, Costanza's manuscript was sent off for peer review; only this time the comments that came back were more favorable.

"It seems to me that this paper does deserve publication," said one reviewer. "I could find no major technical errors." Another reviewer was equally gushing—remember, these are scientists; praise doesn't come easy: "This is a huge effort to tackle an appropriately large subject. It makes for compelling reading. I congratulate the authors on their approach." This reviewer, though, did sound a note of warning for what was to come. "No doubt there will be much nit-picking about particular numbers. As in the largest entries the paper provides a target at which others can shoot."

The paper, "The Value of the World's Ecosystem Services and Natural Capital," was duly published by *Nature* in its May 15, 1997, edition.

Costanza and his colleagues got to publish their estimate of what GDP would look like if it were to be calculated in a different way, and the rest of the world got to hear about it. Because of that, governments are using the methodology Costanza's team used to value environmental services all over the world and have, over the intervening years, been filling in the gaps in the original analysis. The fact that ecological economics alone now has 2,000 scholars from more or less a standing start is no small achievement. And that includes many mainstream economists too.

Thanks largely to Costanza and his colleagues, mainstream economists are more likely to accept that unless the environment has a price tag, unless it is valued, the world will be forced to pay a lot more to replace it.

In the next chapter we will meet one of them.

Ten

Stern Lessons

Those who pollute, should pay.
— President Blaise Compaoré of
Burkina Faso, African Union
heads of state summit (2007)

I n the world of economists, Lord Nicholas Stern is a rock star, a red-carpet-treading member of the A-list. Stern has worked at the top of academia, at the heart of the UK government, and at the World Bank in Washington, DC. Influential at home, he has the ear of leaders from Dallas to Delhi. As a member of the UK House of Lords and president of the British Academy, the body representing leading humanities and social science scholars, Stern's word carries weight.

Nicholas Stern is important to our story because he represents the one constituency that, back in 1997, Robert Costanza and his team of ecological economists found hardest to persuade. Nicholas Stern is an economist of mainstream thought and practice, except that unlike many of his colleagues, he could read both the politics *and* the economics of putting a price tag on nature. After Costanza's $33 trillion estimate for a green-adjusted GDP, it would be Stern's turn to build on the idea of valuing the environment and to take the argument to his mainstream colleagues. But unlike Costanza, Stern also had considerably stronger political firepower at his disposal.

In October 2003 Stern had become head of the UK's Government Economic Service. He had been hired from the World Bank, where he'd been chief economist, and his new boss would be the chancellor Gordon Brown.[1] In that role Stern made a name for himself by successfully steering one of the most complicated mergers in UK civil service history: the union of the government agency that collects income taxes and the agency that is responsible for indirect taxes. "We were 100 years late in doing this," he told me in an interview in June 2014. That project could easily have bombed, but Stern managed to hold it together, and it brought him to the attention of Tony Blair, who was then prime minister.

At the time Blair, Brown, and the two pop-star campaigners Bono and Bob Geldof had set up a body called the Commission for Africa. This was essentially a blue-ribbon committee of Africa's leaders, sitting alongside heads of state and international business leaders. Its aim was to bring more prosperity (including growth) to the countries of Africa.

By the time Nick Stern attracted Blair's attention, the Commission for Africa was having problems in part because of mounting tensions between Blair and Brown.[2] Stern says the final report was "drifting." His appointment to head the project's secretariat, however, was supported by both Blair and Brown, as neither wanted this flagship project to fail. "Initially, Gordon wanted Treasury control over the project but both realized I had no axe to grind. I wasn't part of any camp." Stern told me it took him time to win Geldof's trust, though, as the singer "thought I was some World Bank-type market economist."[3]

As with his previous project in the UK Treasury, Stern delivered the goods. The commission's final report appeared on time and to wide acclaim.[4] Stern did more than deliver for his bosses, however; he also gained Brown's and Blair's trust as a kind of honest broker, and in that sense he was the ideal interlocutor for the warring leaders' next big international project—on climate change.

The last UK Labour government was a quite reforming administration when it came to climate change. Both Blair and Brown accepted the consensus among climate scientists that global warming is happening, that its causes include industrial growth, and that the consequences of business as usual could be severe. Blair oversaw new laws committing the government to tough reductions in greenhouse gas emissions,[5] and when Brown became prime minister he appointed a dedicated minister for climate change.[6]

Blair also knew (or he was advised) that climate protection faced many hurdles, one of which was the view of many of his colleagues that taking action to slow down global warming is essentially bad news for energy security and for jobs: that it is antigrowth. Around Blair's cabinet table, there was only one minister arguing the other way. His long-serving environment minister, Michael Meacher, was often a lone voice in cabinet, though experienced and adept at knowing how to pull the levers of power when he needed to.[7]

The Blair government had decided that something had to be done to persuade the doubters, and on an altogether larger scale than had been tried by individual heads of government before.

◆

At the start of 2005, eight years after Robert Costanza's $33 trillion estimate for an environment-adjusted economy, the UK found itself holding the presidency of two important meetings of heads of government. One was the annual meeting of the leaders of the Group of Eight developed countries, which would be held in Scotland in December. At that time the G8 countries were the United States, France, Germany, China, Canada, Italy, the UK, and Russia. The other presidency was that of the twenty-seven-member European Union.[8] As journalists readied themselves for twelve months of "President Blair" jokes, the man himself was preparing to live up to the name.

International summits of world leaders tend to follow a set formula. The main discussion item is almost always the state of the world economy. However, host nations also like to include one or two extra topics that are of national or global importance, usually on issues that require coordinated global action. At the same time it is no secret that leaders like to put such issues on the agenda to help them appear more statesmanlike when the cameras start to roll.

Choosing topics on which there are strong opinions can be quite a gamble, as the last thing anyone (hosts or guests) wants is a major public disagreement. But in 2005, with the UK hosting not one but two global summits, the UK government chose to roll the dice. It selected African development and climate change as headline topics for the presidencies of both the G8 and the EU,[9] ensuring that both these topics would dominate the global conversation that year. At the same time, there was determination that each event should conclude with practical and concrete outcomes.

For Blair, convincing fellow world leaders to commit more for African trade and development would in hindsight be the easy part. Persuading them that concrete action had to be taken now on climate change would be an altogether different matter, especially for US President George W. Bush. Bush had few problems agreeing to an extra $25 billion in aid for countries in Africa. But Blair wanted Bush to go further: he wanted the G8 meeting to confirm what the overwhelming majority of scientists were saying, that climate change was man-made and that action had to be taken to slow down and eventually reverse carbon emissions. He tried to sell climate change to Bush by warning him that more weather extremes would create more global insecurity and migration. But the more he tried to convince Bush, the more he found Bush retreating. In the end, the G8 leaders decided that on climate change, they would agree to disagree. "To describe George [Bush] as a sceptic would be an understatement," Blair would later write in his memoirs.[10]

UK government advisers knew that in order to make meaningful progress on climate change they needed a body of evidence that would persuade world leaders and their ministries of finance that the advice they were getting was wrong: that delaying action on climate change had consequences for future growth, but also that growing economies can be greener ones, too—essentially the flip side of Robert Costanza's analysis. And to be credible, such a message had to be delivered by an economist with first class credentials.

Tony Blair and Gordon Brown were essentially faced with the predicament Maurice Strong and Aurelio Peccei had confronted four decades earlier. To challenge those who wielded greatest influence in world economic affairs, they had to draw on the voice of empiricism. Once again it was time to call on the services of Nicholas Stern.

◆

Since Maurice Strong's successful stewardship of the 1972 Stockholm summit, and especially in the nearly three decades since the Rio Earth Summit of 1992, governments have become convinced that environmental degradation is real and that something needs to be done to ward off its consequences. However, it is also the case that ministries of trade and ministries of finance are not always in any great rush to agree to action.

Trade ministries are reluctant to support any policy that stops businesses, particularly large multinational businesses, from pursuing their goals. Finance ministries, on the other hand, are skeptical about anything that could interfere with the GDP numbers. For example, if dealing with climate change means people go shopping less, take fewer flights, or use their cars on fewer occasions, then there's no doubt that GDP will be affected.

This was the context in which Nicholas Stern was asked to produce his report on the economics of climate change. He had to convince his colleagues in finance ministries that dealing with climate change doesn't make countries poorer, and he had to find a way to demonstrate that combating global warming might even be good for growth—at least in the long run.

The assignment would perhaps be his toughest yet. The economist in Stern had to master forest ecology, the chemistry of oceans, and the physics of weather systems. He also had to calculate how to place a value on many of the environmental services we currently take for granted. He needed to find out what it would cost if oceans and forests, mountains and lakes, were lost or degraded from climate change.

On October 30, 2006, Stern and his team at the UK Treasury returned with the report that bears his name.[11] The team concluded that if the world's finance ministers all agreed to spend 1 percent of GDP now on measures to tackle global warming, this would save the world economy from bigger falls in GDP in the future. The damage to lives, jobs, and ecosystems from climate change could, according to Stern, lead to a 20 percent fall in consumer spending, for example. "Our main message was that the costs of action are less than the costs of inaction," Stern told me in an interview.[12] "Indeed, doing little is very damaging if not reckless," he added. "And delay matters: the longer you leave things, the worse they will get." It was a memorable line: Spend 1 percent now; save 20 percent later.

Governments publish policy reviews most days of the week. However, a few days before the Stern report's launch I was sensing that this would be a different kind of government document from the usual fare. For one thing, Stern was fortunate in having the combined resources of several UK government departments helping to promote the review and its conclusions. In addition, he was supported by the British Council and by the BBC.[13]

Occasionally, government press officers might leak a snippet or two to help generate advance interest in a forthcoming announcement. But for the Stern review the launch was protected by iron-clad secrecy. Instead, select media were invited to a hotel and given just an hour's access to the document before launch, in a process known as "lock in." That had the effect of adding to the mounting suspense, so that when the story did break, it would be just as big as the publication of Robert Costanza's $33 trillion estimate of world GDP.

Stern lost no time in presenting his conclusions at the highest levels. After UK launch events and back-to-back media interviews, Stern embarked on a tour that would take him to the world's major finance ministries, where he would hold private and public meetings with media, public, and policy makers. I followed the Stern entourage to Ethiopia, Canada, and briefly to Indonesia and saw firsthand the report's extraordinary impact and Stern's elevated status as a mainstream economist who had come in from the cold.

In February 2007, Stern was the guest of the British high commissioner to Canada, Anthony Cary, who also hosted a press conference. This would be followed by a public discussion hosted by the British Council between Stern and Canada's celebrated environmentalist David Suzuki, and a joint statement on climate change released by the British High Commission. As I sat at the back of the hall on a freezing day, I can still recall the delight on Suzuki's face as he greeted Stern with the kind of welcome laid on by religious communities whenever someone famous becomes a convert. Here was Stern, a scion of the economics community, accepting that ecology had a value.

In Ethiopia, however, Stern had a tougher time.

The UK government had arranged for Stern to address the annual meeting of the heads of state of the African Union at the organization's Addis Ababa headquarters in January.[14] At the conference venue I spotted Stern making his way to the room where he would be speaking. But as in Canada he was surrounded by a cordon of officials protecting him from what seemed like hundreds of journalists and members of the public, who all wanted to speak to him.

Stern repeated his report's conclusion—pay 1 percent now to save 20 percent later, but he wisely moderated it for his African audience. He acknowledged that climate change has been caused by the industrialized world and also acknowledged that countries in Africa and in the developing world more broadly will suffer disproportionately unless action is taken soon. He also hinted strongly that rich countries ought to help pay to resolve a crisis that they helped to cause.

Still, not all of the African Union delegates were ready to accept what they were hearing. To some delegates it appeared as if a representative of one of the world's most-polluting nations had come to Africa to lecture the continent's leaders on how to be clean. They interpreted his report as saying, "The developed countries have caused global warming. But the developing countries will stand to lose the most. So my advice to you is to do something about it before it is too late."

Once Stern stood down, Uganda's president, Yoweri Museveni, took the floor. Global warming, Museveni said, is "an act of aggression" by the developed world against the African people. After him, Blaise Compaoré of Burkina Faso declared, "Those who pollute, should pay."[15]

Meanwhile, back home Stern would also begin to feel the heat from mainstream economists from both left and right once they had had a chance to pore over his report in more detail. His most influential critic was Nigel Lawson, long-serving finance minister to Margaret Thatcher. Lawson's position was essentially that of the Conservative government in 1972: the evidence of impending catastrophe is thin, he would tell me in an interview in the summer of 2013. Indeed, global warming could even be good for some northern European countries, as it could boost industries such as wine growing and tourism. On the contrary, according to Lawson, the costs to decarbonize industry are way too high and will make countries such as the UK uncompetitive. "Global warming," Lawson would tell me, "is essentially a religion."[16]

◆

All of this is an echo of Aurelio Peccei's and Maurice Strong's experiences from four decades earlier in the run-up to the 1972 Stockholm environment conference. Now, as before, most of the leaders of both developed and developing nations are not prepared to buy the idea that their citizens would put up with lower growth just so that future generations have a working planet. Additionally, the leaders of developing nations are not prepared to put up with the idea that they must pay for a problem that they did not cause.

Later, Stern would further strengthen his credentials as a green economist by helping to create a $100 billion fund so that developing countries do have the financial resources to deal with climate change. But on the most critical point of all it seems there's been little discernible progress since Stockholm. Valuing the environment is all very well, but if it means harm to countries' growth prospects, then it still constitutes a thick red line.

Something else had to be done to persuade heads of state and governments that growth needs to be about much more than measuring what people and their governments spend. There had to be another way. With Maurice Strong now in his eighties and both Tony Blair and Gordon Brown out of office, the cause would need another champion.

Eleven

"Nothing Is More Destructive of Democracy"

All over the world people believe they are being lied to, that the figures are false; that they are being manipulated. And there are good reasons for feeling this way. For years people whose lives were becoming more and more difficult were being told that living standards were rising. How could they not feel deceived?
— Nicolas Sarkozy, *Mismeasuring Our Lives: Why GDP Doesn't Add Up* (2008)

S hortly after Tony Blair and Gordon Brown's decision to hire Nicholas Stern to guide them through the forest of climate change economics, across the English Channel,

France's president Nicolas Sarkozy announced a project every bit as ambitious. Sarkozy's aim was to take a shot at no less than GDP itself. In doing so he would become the second head of a state to not only realize the problems inherent in GDP, but to take steps to do something about them.

Sarkozy has long believed that GDP does not properly value those aspects of life that French culture both celebrates and is renowned for. A long-held bugbear for France is that GDP ignores, even devalues, those aspects of life that have little or nothing to do with money. As we know, GDP has no category that recognizes happiness or contentment. There is no tick-box or spreadsheet-field that rewards spending time with our families. A parent who chooses to scale back his or her hours, to work part-time, might be good news for the children, but that choice is bad news as far as government growth accountants are concerned.

Sarkozy had a second and possibly more important concern about GDP. Recall the example from Tunisia: in the years leading up to the tragic suicide of Mohamed Bouazizi, Tunisia's economy was celebrated as a regional icon of growth. Successive quarterly announcements of GDP's steady growth masked the gulf in inequality. And recall that in rich countries, rising GDP concealed the continued existence of an underclass. One of the canniest politicians of his generation, Sarkozy believed that the example from Tunisia showed how indicators such as GDP were potentially threatening to nothing less than the survival of democracy.

Here he is in 2008 after the financial crisis, explaining why: "All over the world people believe they are being lied to, that the figures are false; that they are being manipulated. And there are good reasons for feeling this way. For years people whose lives were becoming more and more difficult were being told that living standards were rising. How could they not feel deceived?"[1]

These are the words of a center-right, indeed hawkish head of state, not your average leftish economics blogger. "That is how we create the gulf of incomprehension between the expert certain in his knowledge and the citizen whose experience of life is completely out of synch with the story being told by the data. This gulf is dangerous because the citizens end up believing they are being deceived. Nothing is more destructive of democracy. I hold a firm belief: We will not change our behavior unless we change the ways we measure our economic performance."

GDP, as far as Nicolas Sarkozy was concerned, is on the wrong side of the argument and it had to be reformed.

◆

Sarkozy's first step was a surprising one for someone of his political ilk: this was to meet three respected thinkers broadly on the left of economic policy and establish if they agreed that he was on to something. He called Joseph Stiglitz, the Nobel Prize-winning former adviser to the Clinton administration, and an influential voice in support of policies that reduce inequality. There was Jean-Paul Fitoussi, Sarkozy's economics professor at Sciences Po, the Paris Institute of Political Studies. And finally there was Amartya Sen, coinventor of the Human Development Index and by now a Nobelist, too.

Sarkozy had good reasons for his choice of expert advisers. Joseph Stiglitz has for some years been a leading source for ideas on how to reduce inequality. Fitoussi's value would include acting as cover for Sarkozy against attacks from the home side. Amartya Sen, meanwhile, would bring experience of such an exercise, not to say nearly two decades of reflection on the shaping, launch, successes, failures, and aftermath of the Human Development Index.

In 2007, a whisker before the financial crisis of 2008, Sarkozy asked the trio to gather more of their colleagues, just as Sen and Mahbub ul Haq had done.[2] He requested that they summarize for him the latest thinking in alternative ways to measure economies and societies. This being a political project, the group was given just eighteen months, a far shorter time frame than academics are used to. But crucially for such a project, and just as Blair and Brown had done, the president promised to act on their findings.

Let's for a moment go back to 1989: a buoyant Mahbub ul Haq asks Amartya Sen, his friend from their days as Cambridge students, to join the team that created the HDI. Remember Sen's skepticism, his justified reluctance to join a project to create yet another crude index, with unknown consequences. And remember Haq's reply: that politicians need simplified information. "Amartya," he said, "I want you to create something as vulgar as GDP."

This time, an older, more politically savvy Sen would have it his way.

Mismeasuring Our Lives, as the Sarkozy's commission's final report is titled, makes a thoughtful, careful, and powerfully argued case for what is wrong with GDP and what could replace it. An alternative single number—a composite index collapsing different quantities into one figure—however, is not one of its recommendations.

Mismeasuring Our Lives instead argues for a "dashboard" of indicators that together paint a more accurate picture of a society's well-being. These would include indicators on the living standards of households, such as income, consumption, and wealth. They would also include indicators of health, education, social connections, work, environment as well as insecurity (both physical and economic).[3]

The use of the word "dashboard" is more than a nod to Sen, who has often compared GDP with driving a car using only one instrument showing a spurious reading. And lest anyone had any doubt, the report makes clear to its readers that HDI was one component of a much bigger idea, that it was "the simplest representation" of a broader human development approach that sparked a global revolution in how we measure well-being. Such is their aversion to the single-number idea that no amount of reform, refinement, or improvement is good enough. GDP for Fitoussi, Sen, and Stiglitz is simply not good enough.

The final part of *Mismeasuring Our Lives* also parts company with the more radical thinking of ecological economists, notably Robert Costanza: it rejects ideas to revise GDP, to make GDP more representative of the things that society wants to value. Sarkozy's advisers had no time for an adjusted GDP or a green GDP. And that to my mind was a huge missed opportunity born, it seems, of a reluctance to consider the bigger picture.

One reason why this may have occurred is because Sarkozy's team was insufficiently diverse in its composition of expertise. What I mean here is that the broader group that compiled *Mismeasuring Our Lives* was comprised mostly of economists. In addition there was one political scientist, a sociologist and a psychologist, but no working natural scientist; nor a researcher active in the humanities. Confining themselves to a relatively narrow set of expertise meant that Sen, Stiglitz, Fitoussi and their colleagues were able to reject much of the thinking that had gone into environmental valuation, and to do so without being challenged.

The main reason for their decision seems to be concerns about data accuracy: a reluctance to put a price on something (such as pollution) that isn't bought and sold on an open market. In their view, trying to combine such monetary estimates risked repeating the mistakes of GDP and, not surprisingly, the team recommended that the issue of environmental indicators be parked for a follow-up exercise.

It is difficult to say what Sarkozy made of this, or if indeed he had much sense of the debates and arguments taking place within his report-writing team. He would lose the subsequent general election and his successor, President François Hollande, has shown little interest in giving the project the support that Sarkozy had promised.

But what is certain is that rejecting the idea of a single number, and rejecting ideas around green GDP, hasn't done any favors for the cause of GDP reform. Furthermore, it did not help its patron, Nicolas Sarkozy, should the former president run for office again and pick up from where he left off.

GDP is simply too entrenched as a policy tool to be abandoned just because eminent academics dislike it. And though it is true that in our Big Data world a dashboard of indicators would be easier now than ever to collect and attractive to display, most politicians feel overwhelmed by the quantity of information that they are required to process. For this group of people, a composite index, a single number comprising a range of variables, is, if anything, more needed now than in the past.

Epilogue

Unfinished Revolution

*Most countries have more reliable statistics on
their poultry and egg production than on their
output of discoveries and inventions.*

—Christopher Freeman

All editors of newspapers and magazines have their "golden
rules." These are designed partly to enable publications to
be distinctive, to reflect the values they hold, and to reflect
the values of their readers.

When I edited the Research Professional family of publications, one such rule was never to use the word "foreign" to

describe people who happen not to be citizens of the country where they work. It made no sense because research is a highly mobile profession. The majority of our readers are likely to find themselves working away from their country of citizenship at some point in their careers. Each of us will be foreign at some point in our lives.

Another of our golden rules was to help readers cut through the fog of corporate jargon found in official reports and press releases. Often this is just the result of lazy writing, but words can also be used deliberately to convey ideas that can be laden with baggage. Editorial colleagues would be advised, for example, to think carefully before using the word "investment" in their articles, particularly when it comes to reporting stories about new government funding schemes.

This might seem a small, perhaps trivial point, but it isn't. We need to be cautious because governments have become fond of using "investment" when they really mean "funding," and the two are not the same.

Investment is more often associated with business (as we know from the GDP formula). When businesses invest, they do so because they expect a return on their investment; they expect to make more money than they put in. When governments, on the other hand, provide "funding," they are doing so as part of their role to protect citizens and give them opportunities to prosper. When governments provide funding to upgrade a hospital, resurface potholes on a street, or open a new university lab, that isn't an investment, because they expect no monetary return. Government funding is part of the state's bargain to protect those who elect them and contribute their hard-earned money in the form of taxation.

Governments fund; businesses invest. Or so I thought.

In April 2013, in the midst of writing this book, a headline from the *Financial Times* told me that governments who declare science spending as "investments" *did* have a basis to use that word. I also learned that what I was reading was to have profound implications for how we construct GDP and for ongoing efforts to reform it.

I discovered that it is actually possible to change GDP.

❖

The *Financial Times* story was on the inside pages of my morning read and the headline was simple enough: "Data Shift to Lift US Economy 3%."[1] The *FT* announced to the world that, more or less overnight, the size of the US economy had increased and that this was partly because of a change to how GDP is calculated.

That change involved a kind of arcane accounting trick: it meant moving the column that contains spending on science to a different place in the GDP table. Up until then, everything that businesses and governments spent on science had been regarded as an expense with no expectation of financial return, in the same way that governments spend on hospitals or schools. But now, according to the *FT* article, science spending would be moved to the "investment" column. The reason for this shift was because of a belief, increasingly common among some economists and more politicians, that spending on science makes money. That is certainly true of science spending by businesses, which in rich countries constitutes the majority of science spending. However, it is more controversial than that.[2]

This change to how GDP is worked out had better consequences for those nations with big science budgets and big multinational companies. Countries such as the United States, Britain, Germany, and France would see their GDP revised upward by between 1 and 3 percent.[3] Countries with much more modest research spending and few if any multinational corporations (essentially most of the rest of the world) would see little or no increase.

◆

One of the frustrations of writing this book has been seeing how the struggles of so many great talents had so little effect on changing GDP. Mahbub ul Haq probably came closest to creating an effective global alternative to GDP in the Human Development Index, but this had zero effect on GDP itself. Maurice Strong tried to circumvent the problem by creating an elaborate infrastructure of environmental checks and balances, which did more to raise awareness of GDP's limitations but did not tackle its problems head-on. Meanwhile, Bhutan's fourth king Wangchuck tried to steer his economy using Gross National Happiness alongside GDP. But none, it seems, had given due thought to the elephant in the room. Only Robert Costanza had showed the world what the numbers would look like if GDP could change to stand for better things. Only he was unable to show how to get there.

What few of us knew or understood is that the change to how GDP is calculated that the *FT* was reporting did not happen overnight. It was the culmination of a decades-long effort spearheaded largely by the developed countries and led by their trading club, the OECD. That *FT* story confirmed something known to its practitioners, which is that GDP has been modified—we also know this from the published revisions to its methodology since the 1950s. But the fine-grained process of *how* this has happened, and, more important, the politics of how change was brought about, remains opaque to the general reader, as there is comparatively little scholarship and even less journalism around these issues.

That *FT* story gave me a window of opportunity to try to resolve that question. The rest of this chapter summarizes my attempts to discover how GDP can change.

◆

The story of how the OECD member states, and especially those who were research-intensive economies, succeeded in making a change to the composition of GDP starts half a century earlier and involves two of the characters we've already met in this book.

One was Alexander King, the urbane British civil servant, the first director of science in the OECD. King teamed up with the former Fiat motor industrialist Aurelio Peccei and cofounded an influential club of world leaders they called the Club of Rome. One of their first acts was to commission scientists to create computerized forecasts of environmental collapse, which became *The Limits to Growth* in 1972.

The other was Christopher Freeman, the charismatic University of Sussex economist who was so upset by this idea that he published a stinging rejoinder, *Models of Doom*.

In 1962 Alexander King and Chris Freeman worked closely together on a very different project, which (at least for King) was a polar opposite to his later work on *The Limits to Growth*. In contrast to his later incarnation as a skeptic, King was a GDP enthusiast during his OECD days and in fact hired Freeman as a consultant to create a similar accounting system for science spending.

King had been watching closely how GDP was shaping up. As a highly experienced civil servant he understood one of GDP's great strengths: when something is quantified and valued, and then written up in bright neon lights, it is more likely to be recognized and protected. Most countries in the 1960s, even wealthy ones, were not in the habit of producing accurate accounts of how much they spent, say, on physics projects versus chemistry. King, in his role as head of the science section at the OECD, began to encourage them to do so. At the same time, the OECD itself started publishing league tables of which countries spent the most on their science as a fraction of their GDP.

King and his OECD colleagues also understood something else. Scientists then (and even now) frequently justified their taxpayer dollars and pounds by arguing that all of the leading civilizations needed and funded researchers. King understood that such arguments don't always wash with ministries of finance. He knew that scientists needed to prove to their governments that money spent on science wasn't simply a way to fund generous retirement pensions for professors; it was benefiting the economy too.[4]

King figured correctly that if nations wanted to protect their science spending, they had to find ways to get science mentioned and discussed at the top table of economic policy making, and that would entail adopting some of the language of GDP.

And that is where Chris Freeman came in.

At the request of the OECD, Freeman created an accounting manual for science that helps countries work out how much money goes to different research fields and how much of this spending is helping boost economic growth. This has come to be known as the Frascati Manual (named after the small town near Rome where the first meeting was held). At this event, held in June 1963, Freeman is reported to have said, "Most countries have more reliable statistics on their poultry and egg production than on their scientific effort and their output of discoveries and inventions," and he recommended that countries should be spending at least 3 percent of their GDP on research, because spending on research helps to boost growth.[5]

We know from at least that time that the United States wanted science spending to be included in the GDP accounts as an investment. And we know that the United States had good reasons for this. Two thirds of America's research spending comes from industry, and most of this takes place inside the large multinational corporations, which we know well. For companies such as AT&T, Boeing, Ford, General Electric, and IBM, a dollar spent on research was very much an "investment," because it more than paid for itself in sales of aircraft, cars, and computers and the profits that accrued from these sales. For America's landmark corporations of the 1960s and 1970s, it made perfect sense to regard what is known as Research and Development as an investment.

But Richard Stone and his successors handling GDP methodology initially resisted these efforts, not only to classify science spending as an investment, but also to split the science spending figures in a more granular way, and they had equally good reasons for doing so. They knew, first, that research spending in the rest of the world did not (does not) fit the US model: spending on research does not automatically lead to companies making money and therefore achieving higher levels of growth. Apart from a small number of developed countries and the larger emerging economies, science spending in much of the rest of the world is on a much smaller scale and tends to be dominated by the state. Back in the 1960s and 1970s, even the larger developing countries, such as Brazil, China, and India, mostly funded their scientific research from public sources. They did not have research-intensive multinational corporations of the kind we see today. Reclassifying Research and Development from a cost to an investment for these countries therefore would leave no tangible benefit to their national income.

Furthermore, Stone and his colleagues also knew there was an additional problem, and that had to do with data quality.[6] Most countries do not accurately measure their science spending to the fine-grained level achieved in richer countries. Countries such as the UK, for example, know precisely how much is spent on physics, how much on the humanities, how much on environmental science. They are also careful to separate research spending that is research for its own sake and research spending that might lead to profits. But outside of a handful of OECD countries, science spending is calculated in a far coarser way. It is usually a single lump sum, often thrown in as part of a larger budget for higher education. Moreover, richer countries don't collect such data on a quarterly basis, which is what GDP requires. You can see the problems. National statisticians such as Richard Stone were worried that insisting that all of research contributes to GDP growth would open the door to reams and reams of unreliable data. And he wasn't wrong.

Still, the OECD and the more developed nations didn't give up, and by 1993 they had persuaded the UN to include R&D statistics inside what are called "satellite accounts." Satellite accounts are a very interesting phenomenon. They're a kind of voluntary arrangement whereby national statistics offices promise to start gathering data in an area that governments have begun to regard as important—but not important enough to include in the main GDP accounts. Often, statisticians will use satellite accounts to test whether a lesser-known set of indicators could conceivably make it into the main accounts, as is presently happening with various environmental indicators. Sometimes they're useful for kicking an unwelcome set of indicators into the long grass. But for a determined government, satellite accounts are the perfect launchpad from which to move something into the main GDP index, which is precisely what the United States and its allies (including Britain) did next.

At the same time that science spending moved into the satellite accounts, a number of the OECD's research-intensive member states continued to work together. They created a group called the Canberra Working Group, and after many meetings, in 2007 it was agreed that science spending would in the future be treated as an investment and not as an expense. Australia was the first nation to amend its GDP, and it was followed shortly by Canada, Israel, Mexico, and the United States.[7]

◆

Buried in this story are important lessons for those seeking to change GDP so that it can measure the things that matter to us all. Environmental indicators have made it to the satellite accounts, the outer circle of GDP, just as Research and Development indicators had in 1993. As is the case with science spending, environmental indicators have been part of the satellite accounts for some years. However, the next stage, the jump from the periphery into the main GDP index, could be more difficult unless their proponents understand two realities.

The first is that getting GDP to recognize environmental costs and benefits is not primarily an issue of data quality. Yes, it is true that much of the opposition to the idea that environmental services can be valued in dollars rested on concerns about the quality and accuracy of the figures. And yes, the data does need to get more accurate. Ecological economist Robert Costanza's many critics repeatedly challenged his team to explain how it's possible to accurately value something, such as an ocean or a forest, for which there isn't an army of buyers and sellers, and which isn't traded on the market. Costanza, who famously valued the world's ecosystem goods and services at $33 trillion, responded by asking why the same concerns aren't raised for other components of GDP. GDP's data quality problems are now legion. But how is it, Costanza asked, that GDP has been allowed to reign supreme for eight decades in spite of them.

We already know that GDP still has to find a way to value volunteering and housework; and we know that many countries still lack the tools to properly measure even its existing components. Even when it is first published, GDP is often revised the following quarter when more accurate figures become available. And we can say with some confidence that serious concerns about data quality did not prevent science spending from moving from the periphery of GDP and into the center.[8]

The recapitalization of science spending as an investment happened *in spite of* continuing concerns about data quality. Most countries do not account for their research spending by individual topics or disciplines. Most countries to this day still do not have the capability to distinguish spending for research that is intended to push the boundaries of knowledge and spending for research that is intended to make money. The change happened in spite of the fact that there is little or no benefit for most countries' GDP. Moving science to the investment column in countries with low levels of R&D spending and weak data-collection systems won't boost their GDP.

Costanza was right, but his observation was in fact a convenient distraction for his critics because data quality isn't the main issue. We know from the case of science spending being reclassified as an investment that data-quality concerns are not a primary reason not to change GDP. Most countries of the world *still* do not collect R&D statistics with anything like the accuracy or the granularity of the OECD nations. But that didn't prevent a change from happening—a change that everyone needs to implement, regardless of the quality of their data sets or the quality of their data-gathering processes.

The second lesson is to recognize that GDP change will need campaigners to change their approach. Right now perhaps a majority in the environmental community are more supportive of the idea of a dashboard of indicators, including environment, health, and well-being. They remain opposed to a single index and cannot see themselves effectively endorsing a principle they are so opposed to. They are of course right to be skeptical, but they could perhaps reflect on the reasons why so much environment policy they have helped to create has had relatively little real impact. One of these reasons remains the dominance of GDP. If they want to move the world onto a greener path, they will need to engage with GDP's processes just as much as they do for climate change.

The final lesson is that no revision of GDP can afford to ignore the interests of powerful nations, and especially the United States and China. Nearly fifty years ago the British economist Dudley Seers (and others) was spot-on when he said measurement systems tell you as much about the motives of their designers as they do about what is being measured.

Let's go back to the original question of why GDP became mainstream in the first place. GDP became mainstream because, as Seers reminded us, it was designed with the interests of rich countries in mind. After the end of World War II, the forerunner to the OECD promoted GDP as a system of accounting to reassure richer nations that the assistance they were providing under the Marshall Plan wasn't being misspent and was contributing to the growth of economies. Seers and Mahbub ul Haq both understood that GDP, at its core, wasn't really about benefiting developing countries at all, but they still had no choice but to implement it.

That is why any revision to the index won't pass muster unless the interests of its founder countries are protected. And first and foremost that means that any revision must not result in a downward slide; any revision to growth cannot result in the large economies shrinking. It doesn't matter so much if the quality of the data is a bit ropy. What matters more is that countries that are permanent members of the UN Security Council will not allow a change to GDP that leads to them slipping down the league table.

Perhaps Mahbub ul Haq's greatest error when devising the Human Development Index is that he allowed the United States to slide down the rankings. This was an error he quickly realized and corrected, though by then the damage had been done. Although he fought hard to protect the index team from being interfered with by governments, and especially by the US government, Haq's victory may well have been pyrrhic. The US administration probably never forgave him for the humiliation of a lowly position in the first HDI tables.

Paradoxically, this error keeps being repeated by the many alternative accounting systems that have been developed since. If valuing the environment or quality of life means richer nations drop down the index, they simply won't allow the change to happen.

Haq's heirs cannot afford to make the same mistake again.

The End of the Word

A Note on Symbols

G DP comprises six symbols. It looks like a formula from mathematics. It has the elegance and the aura of being an equation, yet it isn't one. As we saw in Chapter 2, the idea didn't even need to be expressed in this way. Indeed, it wasn't, not by Simon Kuznets, not by John Maynard Keynes. National income accounting was represented by both men as a table with different columns for different kinds of spending. The symbols came later.

Had GDP remained expressed as a table, with each form of spending confined to its own column, I do sometimes wonder whether the idea of running the world's economies through a single number would ever have taken off. That it did owes as much to the trend across the humanities and social sciences to adopt math-like notation, a way for such ideas to appear more "scientific." The real language of science—hypothesis, experimentation, testing—was not so much the objective as was scientific notation.

And as we know, such use of specious mathematical notation has contributed to some of the most dangerous ideas in recent decades. One of these is the infamous Gaussian copula, a financial engineering formula widely used by banks and their regulators to predict the level of mortgage default. The formula was popular among finance professionals, as they believed it would enable them to predict a borrower's creditworthiness without having to use actual financials. But until the crash of 2008, no one questioned the soundness or otherwise of the underlying data on which it was based.[1]

In the pre-Gaussian days a bank trying to establish whether a mortgage applicant was creditworthy would look at the applicant's financial history. The bank manager would see what the applicant had borrowed and find out if he or she had defaulted in the past. The bank would know something about the applicant—his or her job or business, perhaps more. Only then would the bank know if it was safe to hand out a large loan.

Now, armed with the formula, banks happily lent money to people in no position to repay their loans. They did so, reassured that the Gaussian copula was telling them the chances of default would be slim. By the end of 2001 the market in mortgage-backed securities, known as credit default swaps, was $920 billion. By the end of 2007 it had shot to $62 trillion. When the following year account holders did start to default on their loans, the banks lost trillions of dollars and governments had to step in to bail them out in what we now know to have been the globe's most serious financial crisis since the 1930s.

◆

The use of x and y to denote unknown quantities is relatively recent, at least as deep history goes. You won't have been taught this in school mathematics, but until the 1500s algebra was written down using words.[2]

Historians say that the trend for writers to use symbols for "plus" and "minus" began from around 1400. Symbols such as those used for "equals," multiplication, and division found use between 1525 and 1687 with the publication of Isaac Newton's *Principia*. Interestingly, many of the symbols we now use in everyday arithmetic were conceived and adopted in this relatively short 150-year spurt.[3]

That isn't the full story, however, as it doesn't explain how symbols became mainstream in writing, teaching, and research in the social sciences and humanities. For that we need to fast-forward another century and dive briefly into the world of university exams.

These days, we know that exams, whether in schools or universities, involve large groups of candidates, sitting hunched over desks, rapidly writing essays or, more often, completing multiple-choice questions under timed conditions under the watchful eye of a teacher. And yet this is not how students used to be assessed. Up until the early 1800s, there were few if any exams of the kind we know today. Instead, students intending to graduate from universities had to pass an oral test, known as viva voce, or "living voice."

The viva voce consisted of a student standing in front of a class of peers and being questioned by his professors. The purpose of the test was to examine the students' ability to reason, to construct a sound argument in support of an idea. Students were also assessed on their confidence as public speakers. Examiners would come prepared to attack a candidate's learning, often using dubious arguments, and successful graduates had to confidently defend themselves.

There are undoubtedly many reasons why students would have been assessed in this way. One reason would have been because pen, ink, and paper were expensive and not yet being produced in enough quantities to bring prices down. Perhaps a more important reason was because of differing expectations of higher education. A university education in most countries until the 1800s was almost exclusively for the elite. If you were lucky enough to bag a place at a university, this was either in preparation for a life spent governing lesser beings in politics or in the church or to build the kind of elite network for which elite universities are still known.

Whether your destiny was to become a country parson or a member of Parliament, there was little point (then) in testing your ability to reel off a list of factoids. Examinations had to be a different kind of test, of knowledge and wit; of public speaking; of the ability to construct and defend an argument, think critically, and think on one's feet. The viva voce was applied across the range of subjects, from theology to mathematics.

The viva voce method undoubtedly benefited those candidates who could handle and learn from an experience where their ideas would be pulled apart in public. And because the entire exercise took place in public, with other students in the audience, it benefited less able students too, as they could watch and learn from their better-performing peers.

With ever larger numbers of students entering universities, professors were demanding a more industrial-scale system. The great virtue of the modern examination is that in one three-hour sitting, hundreds of students can be assessed all at once. But there were implications for the change, and not all have been positive.

On the plus side in mathematics, for example, a largely written test meant an acceleration of the use of written symbols and a more harmonized syllabus. But on the minus side, written exams also meant that students would be assessed more on their memory and recall and less on public speaking, verbal reasoning, and being able to think quickly on their feet. A written exam was clearly testing different things than an oral one.

Equally, the move toward assessing mathematics and science with pen-and-paper exams favored a different type of learner. Someone with strong powers of recall, someone good at taking an accounting approach to mathematics, someone better suited to linear explanations, would do well. Candidates better at taking risks, comfortable with argument, able to hold different points of view at the same time, able to think more holistically, more systemically, would struggle.

Keynes as we have seen was deeply skeptical of the over-mathematization of economics. So concerned was he that, though seriously ill and with weeks to live, he took time out to plead with the Royal Statistical Society not to award a new qualification in statistics, fearing that this would institutionalize what to him was an inferior approach to making decisions.[4]

In recent years, a few eminent academics such as the economist Paul Krugman[5] and the ecologist E. O. Wilson[6] have warned against the over-mathematization of their respective fields. But they remain a minority and to some extent marginal voices. Given the explosion of data and the tools with which to manipulate data, the trend is completely in the other direction.

Our world today is what Keynes feared it would become. Most scientists and economists rely heavily on numerical and statistical models. Pick a country—any country in the world—and its economy, as well as its financial systems, is likewise built on such models. Some of these models, such as GDP, are simplistic. Others, such as those used in banking, can be far more complex. In either case, there are few practitioners who now have the ability to explain, rationalize, or critique using non-mathematical language what they do and why they do it. Of those who can, many are unable to do so using language that all of us can understand.

This is dangerous. It is dangerous for decision making and dangerous for democracy. It is well known that policy made using information accessible only to closed groups of people is often of a poorer quality compared with policy made in an open and consultative way. Moreover, if fewer and fewer of us really understand the workings of policies that affect our lives, there can be little doubt that we will have much less faith and much less trust in the process by which those decisions are made.

When Keynes died peacefully on Easter Sunday in 1946, the world lost a powerful and influential critic of linear thinking and specious symbols. It is time for a new generation to return to his cause and to win it.

ACKNOWLEDGMENTS

I am indebted to a large number of people without whose generous time and selfless cooperation this book would not have been possible.

For the first edition, I would like to acknowledge Claiborne Hancock of Pegasus Books in New York City for seeing the book's potential after a first reading of a manuscript draft; Kirsty Irving and Barbara Izdebska for inspired picture research; Eileen Chetti for careful editing; and Maria Fernandez for classy design and layout. Thanks also to Alia Masood for introducing me to the work of the conceptual artist Miriam Sugranyes who did such great work on the original jacket.

I am also very grateful to all those who gave up time for interviews, in some cases over the course of several years. In particular, they are: Bob Costanza whose 1997 *Nature* paper, "The Value of the World's Ecosystem Services and Natural

Capital," planted a seed for this book, and Herman Daly, who walked me through the birth pangs of ecological economics. I am also grateful to the late Maurice Strong who helped me to reconstruct the 1972 Stockholm environment conference and to Roberto Peccei who spoke movingly about his late father Aurelio.

Lord Meghnad Desai, Bill Draper, Sir Richard Jolly and Frances Stewart illuminated the early years of the Human Development Index and Richard especially provided detailed comments on an early draft of the manuscript. Many thanks also go to Dasho Karma Ura who described the making of Gross National Happiness; to Gustav Papanek for his memories as an economic development consultant in 1950s Karachi; and to Lord Nicholas Stern for re-living both the Commission for Africa and the Stern review on the economics of climate change. A huge thanks also to Kate Pickett, co-author of *The Spirit Level*, for the generous cover quote.

You would think that our digital age would mean less work for librarians and archivists, but I can assure readers that their services remain much sought after. I am especially grateful to Kate Mollan of the National Archives and Records Administration in Washington DC for dogged pursuit of an original copy of Simon Kuznets's 261-page report *National Income 1929–32*; and to the staff at the library of the Institute of Development Studies in Sussex for material on Dudley Seers. Many thanks also go to the development economist Khalid Ikram and to Javed Jabbar, a onetime minister in two Pakistani governments. They helped me to locate the original text of Mahbub ul Haq's landmark "Twenty-two families" speech to the (formerly) West Pakistan Management Association in 1968. It was a privilege to be invited to address the now Pakistan Management Association's 2018 convention in Karachi.

ACKNOWLEDGMENTS

Many wonderful individuals enabled me to test preliminary ideas and conclusions, and helped in other ways, too. James Wilsdon, who chaired an influential report on the use of metrics in British science, invited me to speak to a gathering of economists at the University of Sussex; Julia Marton-Lefèvre extended invitations to address colleagues at the headquarters of the International Union of Conservation of Nature (IUCN) in Gland, Switzerland and also to Maurice Strong's 80th birthday celebrations. Martin Rose and Mike Hardy, two former stalwarts of the British Council, generously invited me to give lecture tours of Canada and Indonesia; and my daughter Huda Masood helped me explore Buddhism's links to conservation.

Three colleagues from science journalism deserve a special mention. Henry Gee and Laura Garwin actively fuelled my interest in ecological economics. Michael Bond provided valuable comments on an earlier manuscript, as did a fourth colleague, Peter Tallack, founder of The Science Factory literary agency. This is our third book together, and I am much looking forward to the next adventure.

An author's craft is often honed at the expense of family commitments. In the year before (and after) publication, I am, and will remain especially grateful to Alya, Huda, Hibah, Danyal, and Hana for tolerating past and future absences.

Finally, I have learnt an incalculable amount from three natural born empiricists with a parallel gift for political insight, or what William Petty might have meant when he coined the phrase "Political Arithmetick." They are: my father Hassan Masood, an Associate of the Institute of Actuaries; William Cullerne Bown, chairman and publisher of Research Professional; and the late David Dickson, founding director of SciDev. Net and my longtime editor at *Nature*.

None of those mentioned carries any responsibility for the content of what appears between the covers of this book.

NOTES

PREFACE TO THE SECOND EDITION

1   IMF World Economic Outlook, October 2020: https://www.
     imf.org/en/Publications/WEO/Issues/2020/09/30/world-
     economic-outlook-october-2020#Full%20Report%20and%20
     Executive%20Summary (accessed 21 December 2020).

2   Working paper from Martin de Ridder of the University
     of Cambridge: http://covid.econ.cam.ac.uk/de-ridder-
     government-expenditures-during-coronavirus-pandemic
     (accessed 17 December 2020.

3   G. Ceballos, P. R. Ehrlich, P.H. Raven, "Vertebrates on the
     brink as indicators of biological annihilation and the sixth mass
     extinction," *Proceedings of the National Academy of Sciences*, June
     2020, 117 (24) 13596–13602; DOI: 10.1073/pnas.1922686117
     (accessed 4 January 2021).

4   For an assessment of the relationship between biodiversity and pandemics, see this review from the Intergovernmental Science-Policy Platform on Biodiversity and Ecosystem Services (accessed 4 January 2021): https://ipbes.net/sites/default/files/2020-12/IPBES%20Workshop%20on%20Biodiversity%20and%20Pandemics%20Report_0.pdf.

5   Jonathan Haskel and Stian Westlake explain how economic growth metrics undervalue the tech giants' contributions to growth in their book *Capitalism Without Capital* (Princeton, NJ: Princeton University Press, 2018).

6   D. Coyle, B. Mitra-Kahn, *Making the Future Count*, Indigo Prize-winning essay, 2017: http://global-perspectives.org.uk/wp-content/uploads/2017/10/making-the-future-count.pdf (accessed 12 December 2020).

7   G. Daily, J. Liu, Z. Ouyang et al, "Using Gross Ecosystem Product to Value Nature in Decision-Making," *Proceedings of the National Academy of Sciences,* June 23, 2020, 117 (25), 14593–14601: https://doi.org/10.1073/pnas.1911439117 (accessed 12 December 2020).

8   *The Financial Times*, December 23, 2020, "Time for a New Approach to Growth": https://www.ft.com/content/a790e713-d942-438d-885c-6b393e97e0e4 (accessed 1 January 2021).

9   See for example World Economic League Table from the Centre for Economic and Business Research: https://cebr.com/service/macroeconomic-forecasting/ (accessed 1 January 2021).

10   *The Economist*, May 13, 2017, "In the Name of GDP: In China, a TV soap on corruption attracts a mass following."

11   Wang Jinnan, "Revive China's Green GDP Programme," *Nature*, 534, 37 (2016): https://www.nature.com/articles/534037b (accessed 12 December 2020).

12   Jacob Assa and Ingrid Harvold Kvangraven, "Imputing Away the Ladder: Implications of Changes in GDP Measurement for Convergence Debates and the Political Economy

of Development," *New Political Economy*, 2021; DOI: 10.1080/13563467.2020.1865899 (accessed 10 January 2021).

13   United Nations Statistical Commission Report on the 51st session (March 3–6, 2020), Economic and Social Council, Official Records, 2020, Supplement No. 4: https://unstats. un.org/unsd/statcom/51st-session/documents/2020-37-FinalReport-E.pdf (accessed 12 December 2020). If, for example, a housing developer has cleared a forest to build homes, the government will need to do two things when including this in GDP. Firstly, as expected, it will add up the economic value of the new homes, which usually leads to GDP going up. But, for the first time, it will also need to subtract the value of all those previously free services that the forest would have provided to humans, such as the value of water purification, carbon capture, and the value of the forest as a place of recreation. This second calculation is likely to reduce GDP.

PREFACE

1.   My Pakistan economics lessons took place in a small, newly opened independent college called the Centre for Advanced Studies, established by the radical education reformer Sami Mustafa. Mustafa had come back to Pakistan after a spell studying and teaching in the United States, determined to make a difference in an otherwise lackluster education system. His college is still going strong.

2.   In *GDP: A Brief but Affectionate History* (Princeton, NJ: Princeton University Press, 2013), Diane Coyle, professor of economics at the University of Manchester, says that GDP can be measured in three ways. The first is by adding up everything that an economy *produces*. The second is by adding together *spending* (or expenditures). The third method is to calculate *incomes*. Offices for national statistics in most

countries will report on the results of all three methods. In the 1930s, Colin Clark and Simon Kuznets favoured an incomes approach. Much of the global media at the time of writing concentrates on the expenditures approach. This book will do the same, that is to define GDP as the sum of all that is spent in the domestic economy, unless specified otherwise. Occasionally, readers may see the letters GNP, or Gross National Product. The difference between GDP and GNP is that the latter also includes economic activities of national entities overseas. In many countries, including the United States, the difference between the two can be significant.

INTRODUCTION: THE GREAT INVENTION

1. J. Steven Landefeld, "GDP: One of the Great Inventions of the 20th Century," *Survey of Current Business*, Bureau of Economic Analysis, January 2000, 6.

2. William M. Daley, "Press Conference Announcing the Commerce Department's Achievement of the Century," *Survey of Current Business*, Bureau of Economic Analysis, January 2000, 10.

3. Jan Luiten van Zanden, Joerg Baten, Marco Mira d'Ercole, Auke Rijpma, Conal Smith and Marcel Timmer, *How Was Life: Global Well-Being Since 1820* (Paris: OECD Publishing, 2014), 64.

4. Alan Greenspan, "Press Conference Announcing the Commerce Department's Achievement of the Century," *Survey of Current Business*, Bureau of Economic Analysis, January 2000, 12.

5. Josiah Stamp, "The Measurement of National Income," in *Wealth and Taxable Capacity: The Newmarch Lectures for 1920–1 on Current and Statistical Problems in Wealth and Industry* (London: P. S. King & Son, 1922), 39.

6.   Khadija Haq and Richard Ponzio, *Pioneering the Human Development Revolution: An Intellectual Biography of Mahbub ul Haq* (New Delhi: Oxford University Press, 2008), 101

ONE: GDP AND ITS DISCONTENTS

1.   See Author's Note (note 2).

2.   GDP does not include government spending known as "transfer payments," such as welfare or pensions.

3.   Charles Bean, "Independent Review of UK Economic Statistics: Interim Report," HM Treasury, December 2, 2015, accessed December 8, 2015, https://www.gov.uk/government/publications/ independent-review-of-uk-economic-statistics-interim-report.

4.   My high school economics teachers in the UK were Ian Pinkus and John Dickinson and they taught at what is now Coombe Boys School, New Malden, Surrey. Re-reading their notes I can see that they took a playful approach to teaching what could have been a dry topic. They defined GDP as a collection of goods and services measured in terms of money. The definition came with a series of health warnings regarding the difficulties in measurement. These difficulties included incomplete information—"Some items have to be estimated, e.g., when a dressmaker does a job for a friend." International comparisons of GDP, they added, are "pretty useless" because different countries have different needs and different ways of measuring well-being and prosperity. Finally, they ended by saying that the figures "cannot measure quality of life, pollution, or the effects of siting cruise missiles next to Newbury Racecourse."

5.   "Gross Domestic Product: Preliminary Estimate, Q2 2012," Office for National Statistics, July 25, 2012, accessed July 31, 2015, http://www.ons.gov.uk/ons/rel/gva/gross-domestic-product--preliminary-estimate/q2-2012/index.html.

6. Russell Lynch, "Work Experience Chancellor George Osborne Urged to Quit as GDP Slumps," *Independent*, July 26, 2012, accessed July 31, 2015, http://www.independent.co.uk/news/uk/politics/work-experience-chancellor-george-osborne-urged-to-quit-as-gdp-slumps-7976829.html.

7. "Labour Market Statistics, August 2012," Office for National Statistics, accessed July 31, 2015, http://www.ons.gov.uk/ons/rel/lms/labour-market-statistics/august-2012/index.html.

8. "Rise in Home Movers Drives Boost in House Purchase Loans and Gross Lending," Council of Mortgage Lenders, September 12, 2012, accessed July 31, 2015, http://www.cml.org.uk/news/press-releases/3302/.

9. "Help to Buy (equity loan scheme) and Help to Buy: NewBuy statistics: April 2013 to December 2014," Department for Communities and Local Government, accessed November 22, 2015, https://www.gov.uk/government/uploads/system/uploads/attachment_data/file/399565/Help_to_Buy_Equity_Loan_and_Help_to_Buy_NewBuy_statistical_release.pdf.

10. Marina Vornovytskyy, Alfred Gottschalck, and Adam Smith, "Household Debt in the US: 2000 to 2011," accessed July 31, 2015, https://www.census.gov/people/wealth/files/Debt%20Highlights%202011.pdf.

11. Gordon Brown, "Budget Statement," *Hansard Parliamentary Debates*, Commons, April 9, 2003, accessed July 31, 2015, http://www.publications.parliament.uk/pa/cm200203/cmhansrd/vo030409/debtext/30409-04.htm. Brown, who was chancellor for ten years, began to develop a habit of repeating how his government was delivering the longest period of continuous economic growth ever recorded.

12. This data comes from the nonprofit organization Trussell Trust, one of the UK's largest providers of emergency food supplies. The charity operates 445 food banks, to which citizens and

businesses donate food, which is then distributed to those in need; www.trusselltrust.org, accessed July 31, 2015.

13. Tunisia page of UN Data, accessed December 3, 2015 http://data.un.org/CountryProfile.aspx?crName=Tunisia. The data shows 17.4 percent unemployment in 2012.

14. Carmen DeNavas-Walt and Bernadette D. Proctor, "Income and Poverty in the United States: 2013," US Census Bureau, September 2014, accessed August 1, 2015, http://www.census.gov/content/dam/Census/library/publications/2014/demo/p60-249.pdf.

15. Johan Rockstrom, Will Steffen, Kevin Noone, Åsa Persson, F. Stuart Chapin III, Eric F. Lambin, Timothy M. Lenton, et al., "A Safe Operating Space for Humanity," *Nature* 461 (2009): 472–475, accessed December 3, 2015, http://www.nature.com/news/specials/planetaryboundaries/index.html. The fossil record suggests the background rate of species loss to be between 0.1 and 1 extinctions per million species per year for marine life, and between 0.2 and 0.5 extinctions for mammals. Today, the rate of species extinction is between 100 and 1000 times more than what could be considered "natural." Human activities, especially urbanization and industrial-scale farming are among the causes.

TWO: THE FIGHT FOR THE FORMULA

1. David Moss and Joseph P. Gownder, "The Origins of National Income Accounting," *Harvard Business Review*, December 30, 1998. This is a Harvard Business School case study in which the authors reproduce three primary documents, including the 1932 US Senate resolution in which Simon Kuznets was commissioned.

2. Carol S. Carson, "The History of the United States National Income and Product Accounts," *Review of Income and Wealth* 21 (1975): 153–181. Carson, a member of the Commerce

Department's Bureau of Economic Analysis, points out that Senator La Follette Jr. was not the only senior official looking for national income data around the time of the Great Depression, and that such an idea was "in the air."

3. Copies of the full 261-page report exist online. However, the National Archives and Records Administration in Washington, DC, has only a six-page summary. Staff told me that for some reason Simon Kuznets's original document was never saved or archived. They added that it is possible that a copy may exist in Senator La Follette's private papers.

4. Carson, "History of the United States National Income," 159.

5. *National Income 1929–32*, Department of Commerce, in response to Senate Resolution No. 220, 72nd Congress (Washington, DC: Government Printing Office, 1934).

6. Benjamin Mitra-Kahn, "Redefining the Economy: How the 'Economy' Was Invented in 1620 and Has Been Redefined Ever Since" (doctoral thesis, City University London, 2011). Mitra-Kahn's account, based on primary sources, says Keynes's contribution to GDP has been overlooked, partly because it "contradicts the official [government] history of a smooth evolution from Kuznets to GNP."

7. Robert Skidelsky, *John Maynard Keynes: The Economist as Saviour 1920–1937* (London: Macmillan, 1992). My reading of Keynes is taken from *The General Theory of Employment, Interest and Money* (New York: Harcourt, Brace & World, 1936) and *How to Pay for the War* (London: Macmillan, 1940), as well as the three volumes of Skidelsky's biography.

8. In response to the 2008 crash, the US Congress authorized $700 billion in "Keynesian" government spending called the Troubled Asset Relief Program, or TARP. Although the program is associated with President Barack Obama, it was in fact President George W. Bush who signed it into law on October 3, 2008. "TARP Programs," US Treasury Department,

accessed August 1, 2015, http://www.treasury.gov/initiatives/
financial-stability/TARP-Programs/Pages/default.aspx.

9. John Kenneth Galbraith, *A History of Economics: The Past as
    the Present* (London: Penguin Books, 1987), 222. Galbraith
    called Hitler a Keynesian before Keynes.

10. In *The Entrepreneurial State*, Mariana Mazzucato, professor
    of economics at the University of Sussex, describes how many
    of the components of Apple's iPhone, for example, would not
    have been available for the company to use had it not been for
    prior government investment in certain technologies.

11. Skidelsky, *Keynes*, 544.

12. Ibid., 540. In fact, as Keynes's biographer Robert Skidelsky
    points out, Keynes believed that economics was addicted to
    what he called "specious precision," attempting to make precise
    and perfect that which in reality is messy and complex. Keynes
    considered economics to be a "moral" science, meaning that
    it needed the exercise of human judgment, supplemented by
    models and data. Most science and economics today works the
    other way around: We reduce complex behaviors to data that
    isn't always sound or rigorous. We apply ever more elaborate
    ways to understand this data. Then we use words to the effect
    that "this data represents such and such reality."

13. John Maynard Keynes, "The Character of the Problem," *How to
    Pay for the War*, (London: Macmillan, 1940), 1. Keynes's articles
    for the *Times* were subsequently republished in this short book.

14. Colin Clark had come to economics by way of a chemistry
    degree at the University of Oxford and a brief period carrying
    out research in physics. A Labour Party supporter for many
    years, he had tried and failed three times to become a member
    of Parliament. Clark's big break came in 1929 when he got a job
    as a special adviser to a sitting Labour MP, William Beveridge.
    He couldn't have chosen better, for this is the same Beveridge
    who would go on to create the postwar welfare state in Britain.

Colin Clark, *The National Income 1924–1931* (London: Macmillan, 1932), and *National Income and Outlay* (London: Macmillan, 1937).

15. Keynes, *How to Pay for the War*, 13.

16. Mitra-Kahn, "Redefining the Economy," 250.

17. See note 2.

18. Mitra-Kahn, "Redefining the Economy," 250.

19. Mitra-Kahn, "Redefining the Economy," 270.

THREE: MADE IN CAMBRIDGE

1. "The Sveriges Riksbank Prize in Economic Sciences in Memory of Alfred Nobel 1984: Richard Stone," accessed August 7, 2015, http://www.nobelprize.org/nobel_prizes/economic-sciences/laureates/1984/.

2. Keynes was a member of what is called The Bloomsbury Set. This was a close group of freethinking writers and artists who lived and worked in the Bloomsbury district of central London in the first half of the 20th century. They also included the novelists E. M. Forster and Virginia Woolf.

3. Richard Stone, "Autobiography," Nobelprize.org, 1984, accessed December 4, 2015.

4. Richard Stone, "The National Income, Output and Expenditure of the United States of America," *Economic Journal* 206–207 (1942): 154–175.

5. John Maynard Keynes, *A Tract on Monetary Reform* (London: Macmillan and Company, 1923), 79–80.

6. Mauro Baranzini and GianDemetrio Marangoni, *Richard Stone: An Annotated Bibliography* (Lugano: Università della Svizzera italiana, 2015), 11, 18.

FOUR: THE KARACHI ECONOMIC MIRACLE

1. For several decades after partition, "Can Pakistan survive?" was a not uncommon question both among international

commentators and inside the nation's own elites, the most famous example being Tariq Ali, *Can Pakistan Survive? The Death of a State* (New York: Penguin, 1983).

2. Sir Richard Jolly, interview with the author, Lewes, West Sussex, May 29, 2013.

3. Mahbub ul Haq, *The Poverty Curtain: Choices for the Third World* (New York: Columbia University Press, 1976), 3. Haq's first book, *The Strategy of Economic Planning: Case Study of Pakistan* (Oxford: Oxford University Press, 1966), is a classical defense of the idea that maximizing GDP is the route to prosperity. In *The Poverty Curtain* Haq reflects on the lessons learned from his period as chief economist to Pakistan's Planning Commission.

4. William Dalrymple, "On the Trail of the White Mughals," *Daily Telegraph*, August 29, 2015.

5. *Economy of Pakistan* (Karachi: Office of the Economic Adviser, Ministry of Economic Affairs, Government of Pakistan, 1950), 333–340.

6. Gustav Papanek, telephone interview with the author, July 21, 2015.

7. Mahbub ul Haq, "An Evaluation of Pakistan's First Five Year Plan," *The Strategy of Economic Planning: Case Study of Pakistan* (Oxford: Oxford University Press, 1966), 136.

8. Haq, *Strategy of Economic Planning*, 35.

9. *Economy of Pakistan*, 397. The late historian of economic growth Angus Maddison is among those who argued that British colonial rule helped in the deindustrialization of India. The wiping out of the Mughal court and its replacement with a new European bureaucracy reduced the home market for luxury handicrafts by 75 percent. The value of domestic manufacturing and exports was around 6.5 percent of national income. Losing that "was a shattering blow to manufacturers of fine muslins, jewellery, luxury clothing and footwear, decorative swords and

weapons," Maddison wrote. Angus Maddison, *Class Structure and Economic Growth: India and Pakistan Since the Moghuls* (London: George Allen and Unwin, 1971), 53–55.

10. Zahid Hussain, "The First Five Year Plan: Size, Objectives and Limitations," *Pakistan Economic and Social Review* 5 (1956): 3, accessed August 17, 2015, http://pu.edu.pk/home/journal/7/ Volume_5_No_1_1956.html.

11. Haq, *Strategy of Economic Planning*, 156.

12. Gustav Papanek, "Confounding the Prophets," *Pakistan's Development: Social Goals and Private Incentives* (Cambridge, MA: Harvard University Press, 1967), 7.

13. The political context would be different. East Pakistan, which had been much neglected by politicians, who were mostly from the west, was calling for a more equitable transfer of resources and more autonomy to run its affairs. The country as a whole changed prime ministers four times in two years before a military coup in 1958 appeared to have brought some stability and predictability to the planning process. "In marked contrast to the first plan, Pakistan's second five-year plan was launched in propitious conditions," Haq wrote in 1963. "The revolutionary regime, which took over in October 1958, had restored political stability in the country, for lack of which the first plan had failed to command wide political or public support." Haq, *Strategy of Economic Planning*, 173.

14. Ibid., 185.

15. Papanek, "Confounding the Prophets," 7.

16. President Eisenhower's visit of December 1959 made it onto the cover of *Life* magazine. The weekly periodical's 6 million subscribers saw him traveling next to Pakistan's president, Field Marshal Ayub Khan, inside a horse-drawn carriage, beaming and waving to the crowds. "Triumph in Pakistan: Ike and President Ayub," Life, December 21, 1959.

17. Gustav Papanek, "The Development Miracle" (speech under the joint auspices of the Pakistani-American Chambers of Commerce and the Asia Society, New York, May 4, 1965).

18. Haq, *Strategy of Economic Planning*, 1.

19. Ibid., 174, 181.

20. *Economy of Pakistan*, 119.

21. Though delivered without a text, the speech was later published as Mahbub ul Haq, "A Critical Review of the Third Five Year Plan," *Management and National Growth: Proceedings of the Management Convention Held at Karachi* (Karachi: West Pakistan Management Association, April 24–25, 1968), 23–33.

22. Khadija Haq was the author of the work on which Mahbub ul Haq's data was based and he credited her in his speech to the West Pakistan Management Association though perhaps a little ungenerously. He said: "Since my wife was associated with some of these studies, I hope this does not make them less reliable!" Haq, "Critical Review of the Third Five Year Plan," 27. Khadija's research had been commissioned by the Pakistan Institute of Development Economics. However, following the publicity surrounding her husband's speech, her publishers decided to spike the resulting paper, which to this day has never been published.

23. Haq, "Critical Review of the Third Five Year Plan," 27.

24. Papanek, *Pakistan's Development*, 67.

25. Lawrence White, "Industrial Concentration and Industrial Economic Power in Pakistan: The 22 Families (plus a Few More)" (Discussion Paper 24, Research Program in Economic Development, Woodrow Wilson School, Princeton University, July 1972), accessed August 18, 2015, http://www.princeton.edu/rpds/papers/WP_024.pdf.

26. Paul Streeten, "Dudley Seers (1920–83): A Personal Appreciation," *IDS Bulletin* 20, no. 3 (July 1989): 26.

27. Dudley Seers, "What Are We Trying to Measure?" special issue on development indicators, *Journal of Development Studies* 8, no. 3 (April 1972): 21.

28. Biplab Dasgupta and Dudley Seers, "Statistical Policy in Less Developed Countries" (report of the conference Statistical Policy in Less Developed Countries, Institute of Development Studies, University of Sussex, May 12–16, 1975).

29. Sir Richard Jolly, interview with the author, Lewes, West Sussex, May 29, 2013.

30. There appears to be some debate over whether Haq said "twenty families" in his speech, or if the number was twenty-two. The published article based on his speech to the West Pakistan Management Association (see note 21) says "top 20 industrial families," but all subsequent references, including Haq's own, are to twenty-two families.

31. Haq, *Poverty Curtain*, 32–33.

FIVE: RED STAR OVER CENTRAL SQUARE

1. Cambridge 2020 election results: https://www.cambridgema.gov/-/media/Files/electioncommission/2020statepresidential/11032020statepresidentialofficialresults.pdf

2. The historian of McCarthyism Ellen W. Schrecker was interviewed for this chapter in 2017. See also *No Ivory Tower: McCarthyism and the Universities* (Oxford: Oxford University Press, 1988).

3. McCarthy, Congress, and the Eisenhower administration focused their early efforts on the State Department, which they were convinced had become infiltrated by communists. Papanek had been working for an agency in the State Department responsible for foreign aid.

4. Interviews with Gustav Papanek between 2016 and 2020, by phone, email, and in person at Legal Seafoods, Cambridge, and twice at his home in Lexington, Massachusetts. At my

invitation, Professor Papanek also gave a talk to students at Boston University on January 22, 2018: https://www.bu.edu/pardeeschool/2018/01/22/bth-the-politics-of-development-research-in-the-mccarthy-era/ (accessed November 16, 2020).

5   David Halberstam, *The Best and the Brightest* (New York: Ballantyne Books, 1992; originally published 1969). In 1954, Halberstam was editor of Harvard's student newspaper *The Crimson* when he dispatched cub reporter Victor McElheny to cover the trial of the Harvard psychologist Leon Kamin, another of McCarthy's victims. McElheny would become a distinguished science journalist and founder of the Knight Science Journalism Fellowship at MIT.

6   For biographical details on Rostow, see David Milne, *America's Rasputin: Walt Rostow and the Vietnam War* (New York: Hill & Wang, 2008), 23–25.

7   According to Rostow's reading of Marx, a feudal or traditional society is one in which a small number of people are very rich. They own property and the means of production, while everyone else works for poverty wages. Sooner or later, the poor become desperate to escape and make a better life for themselves. In some countries these desperate poor have helped to create a socialist economy, where the state allows more people to own property and establish businesses, thereby helping them to become richer. But like the feudal elites, these new rich still need to exploit people by paying them low wages to increase their own profits.

8   W. W. Rostow, *The Stages of Economic Growth: A Non-Communist Manifesto* (Cambridge: Cambridge University Press, 1960).

9   Part one of the trilogy was Rostow's PhD thesis in which he studied the British Industrial Revolution and sought to understand how industrial technology made Britain a world power. This was published as *The British Economy of the*

Nineteenth Century (Oxford: Oxford University Press, 1948). Four years later in 1952 he published the sequel, *The Process of Economic Growth* (New York: Norton, 1952), in which he broke down the steps through which a feudal society can "take off" to becoming an industrial power. One of Rostow's first mentions of take-off can be found in *The Process of Economic Growth*, 19. Take-off is defined as: "An increase in the volume and productivity of investment in a society, such that a sustained increase in per capita real income results."

10   Ibid., 39. In addition to a doubling of investment spending, Rostow has two other preconditions for take-off in this reference. "The development of one or more substantial manufacturing sectors, with a high rate of growth"; and the ability to mobilize capital from domestic sources.

11   Ibid., 170–71.

12   "Rostow on Growth," *The Economist*, August 15 and August 22, 1959.

13   Max Lerner, "Takeoff Road," *New York Post*, November 21, 1960.

14   Walter Millis, "How to Compete with the Russians," *The New York Times*, February 2, 1958. Sir Roy Harrod, "Wealth of Nations", *Financial Times*, April 12, 1960.

15   Mauro Boianovsky and Kevin D. Hoover, "In the Kingdom of Solovia: The Rise of Growth Economists at MIT, 1956–70," *History of Political Economy* 46 (2014): http://public.econ.duke.edu/~kdh9/Source%20Materials/Research/Boianovsky%20and%20Hoover%20Kingdom%20of%20Solovia.pdf (accessed 17 November, 2020).

16   Letter to Walt Whitman Rostow from Richard Nixon, Office of the Vice President, Washington, June 23, 1959.

17   Yuri Zhukov, "Snipes on a Bog," *Pravda*, October 19, 1959. *Pravda*'s review of *Stages* ends with: "Loud as the snipes may

seem in the capitalist bog, praising its advantages, they cannot change the course of life."

18   These remarks and others came during Khrushchev's US visit between September 15–27, 1959. Cited in N. S. Khrushchev, *Let us Live in Peace and Friendship: The Visit of N. S. Khrushchev to the United States* (New York: Crosscurrents Press, 1960).

19   Rostow's account of his trip to Leningrad and Moscow from May 19 to May 26, 1959 is contained in his papers in the archives of the Massachusetts Institute of Technology. His talk, "The Stages of Economic Growth and the Problems of Peaceful Co-Existence," can be accessed at: https://dspace.mit.edu/handle/1721.1/83060

20   The Soviet Union used a different measurement for national income, called net material product. In contrast to GDP/GNP, this excluded the value of most services. Rostow's estimates (and those in the next reference) were adjusted for this difference.

21   Abraham S. Becker, "National Income Accounting in the USSR," in Vladimir G. Treml and John P. Hardt, *Soviet Economic Statistics* (Durham, NC: Duke University Press, 1972), 96. As regards the growth rate, Soviet statistics claimed the economy grew by around 8 percent over the decade between 1955 and 1966. According to Western sources, the Soviet economy grew by around 6 percent between those years, which also mirrored the US growth rate during the same period. Stanley H. Cohn, "National Income Growth Statistics," in Treml and Hardt, *Soviet Economic Statistics*, 123.

22   This account of the International Economic Association meeting to test the claims made in *Stages* comes from the event's proceedings. Rostow somehow managed to install himself as the book's editor. W. W. Rostow (ed.), *The Economics of Take-Off Into Sustained Growth* (New York: St Martin's Press, 1963).

23   Rostow, *The Stages of Economic Growth*, 39.

24   Phyllis Deane and H. J. Habakkuk, "The Take-Off in Britain," in Rostow, *The Economics of Take-Off*, 63–82.

25   Walther Hoffmann, "The Take-Off in Germany," in Rostow, *The Economics of Take-Off*, 95–118.

26   For the official history of MIT's Center for International Studies, see Donald L. M. Blackmer, *The MIT Center for International Studies: The Founding Years 1951–1969* (Cambridge: MIT Center for International Studies, 2002).

27   W. W. Rostow, *The Dynamics of Soviet Society* (London: Secker & Warburg, 1953).

28   Leon Keyserling was appointed chairman of the White House Council of Economic Advisers by President Truman in August 1946 and served in that position until 1953. Growth—using the $C + I + G$ approach—was a major priority for Keyserling following his experiences of the Depression years. He resigned this post during the McCarthyite purge of left-leaning economists from government. See W. Robert Brazelton, "The Economics of Leon Hirsch Keyserling," *Journal of Economic Perspectives* 11, 4 (1997), 189–97.

29   Halberstam, *The Best and the Brightest*, 157

30   Blackmer, *The MIT Center for International Studies*, 224–25.

31   The Ford Foundation, *Annual Report: 1953*, p. 14. Cited in John Bresnan, *At Home Abroad: The Ford Foundation in Indonesia: 1953–1973* (Jakarta: Equinox, 2006), 29.

32   See for example, Benjamin Higgins, "The Indonesia Five-Year Plan: Proposals for Research," MIT Center for International Studies, September 6, 1957: https://dspace.mit.edu/bitstream/handle/1721.1/83047/14815497.pdf?sequence=1&isAllowed=y (accessed November 22, 2020).

33   Bresnan, *At Home Abroad*.

34   Vincent Bevins, *The Jakarta Method: Washington's Anticommunist Crusade & the Mass Murder Program that Shaped Our World* (New York: Public Affairs, 2020).

35   The leaders of newly independent Indonesia had no problem
      knocking on Moscow's doors for help, and Moscow turned
      out to be a generous lender. Between 1959 and 1965 the Soviet
      government provided the country with 789 million roubles of
      aid, mostly as low-interest loans. The vast majority (90 percent)
      would be used to buy military hardware, with 10 percent
      going to economic development assistance—the most that the
      Soviet Union would ever give to a country that wasn't officially
      communist. See Ragna Boden, "Cold War Economics: Soviet
      Aid to Indonesia," *Journal of Cold War Studies* 10, 3 (2008),
      110–28.

36   David Dapice, "An Overview of the Indonesian Economy," in
      Gustav F. Papanek (ed.), *The Indonesian Economy* (New York:
      Praeger, 1980), 3–55.

SIX: THE TALENTED MR. STRONG

1.   Rachel Carson, "Silent Spring," *The New Yorker*, June 16, 1962,
      35.

2.   Cheryll Glotfelty, "Cold War, Silent Spring: The Trope of
      War in Modern Environmentalism," in Craig Waddell, *And
      No Birds Sing: Rhetorical Analyses of Rachel Carson's Silent Spring*
      (Carbondale, IL: Southern Illinois University Press, 2000), 157.

3.   Quoted in Mark Stoll, "Rachel Carson's Silent Spring,
      A Book That Changed The World," (Rachel Carson
      Center for Environment and Society, Virtual Exhibition,
      2012), accessed November 24, 2015, http://www.
      environmentandsociety.org/exhibitions/silent-spring/
      industrial-and-agricultural-interests-fight-back.

4.   Ehsan Masood, "The Globe's Green Avenger," *Nature*, July
      22, 2009, 454–455. This essay was the result of an invitation
      to attend an international conference in Switzerland held to
      celebrate Strong's eightieth birthday. The event, organized
      by his great friend and fellow environmentalist Julia

Marton-Lefèvre, was a reunion of colleagues, friends, and others to whom Maurice Strong has been a mentor over the past fifty years.

5. John Ralston Saul, "Maurice Strong: Environmental Movement Loses a Founding Father," *The Globe and Mail*, November 30, 2015, accessed December 4, 2015, http://www.theglobeandmail.com/news/world/maurice-strong-environmental-movement-loses-a-founding-father/article27524715/.

6. Maurice Strong, *Where on Earth Are We Going?* (New York: Texere Publishing, 2000), 48–49.

7. Ibid., 52.

8. Ibid., 55.

9. Andrew Brown, *Fishing in Utopia: Sweden and the Future That Disappeared* (London: Granta, 2009), 31.

10. The switch to right-hand driving took place on September 3, 1967, or H-Day as it is known in Sweden.

11. In the 1980s, large parts of the developing world were hit by recession and had to borrow from international financial institutions such as the International Monetary Fund and the World Bank. The conditions of lending included the kinds of prescriptions that Mahbub ul Haq had designed for the young Pakistani economy, as these were seen as more favorable for growth to return. Richard Jolly and Frances Stewart were among this policy's more persuasive critics. See Giovanni Andrea Cornia, Richard Jolly, Frances Stewart, *Adjustment with a Human Face: Protecting the Vulnerable and Promoting Growth* (Oxford: Oxford University Press, 1987).

12. Mahbub ul Haq, *The Poverty Curtain: Choices for the Third World* (New York: Columbia University Press, 1976), 107. Haq would openly talk about his belief that the Stockholm conference had a hidden agenda to keep the developing world from industrializing: "There were suspicions that, after a century or

more of accelerated development and technological progress, the Western societies were telling the majority of mankind that they must return to a simple life and try to make a virtue of it." Haq, *Poverty Curtain*, 80.

13. Strong, *Where on Earth Are We Going?*, 120.

14. Ibid., 125.

15. This strategy was agreed at the end of a two-week meeting of experts in July 1971 in the village of Founex close to Lake Geneva. Strong described this meeting as the most important event in the run-up to the main conference. Haq was the meeting's rapporteur. Stanley Johnson, *UNEP: The First 40 Years* (Nairobi: UNEP Publishing, 2012), 13. The full text of the Founex report can be downloaded from http://www.mauricestrong.net/index.php/the-founex-report, accessed August 18, 2015.

16. While Maurice Strong regards co-opting Mahbub ul Haq as an important success, Haq himself wasn't quite convinced that the conference had been worthwhile and called it "a bit of a disappointment despite the most imaginative efforts of Maurice Strong and Barbara Ward to save it." Haq, *Poverty Curtain*, 81.

17. Maurice Strong, interview with the author, President Hotel, Russell Square, London, 2009.

18. *The Human Environment: The British View, Report Prepared on the Occasion of the Stockholm Conference on the Human Environment* (London: Her Majesty's Stationery Office, 1972), 39.

19. Maurice Strong, interview with the author, President Hotel, Russell Square, London, 2009.

20. Lord Zuckerman, "Science, Technology and Environmental Management," in *Who Speaks for Earth?*, edited by Maurice Strong (New York: W. W. Norton and Co., 1972), 137.

21. Barbara Ward, "Only One Earth," in Strong, *Who Speaks for Earth?*, 22.

22. Roberto Peccei, telephone interview with the author, London, September 9, 2013.

23. Calling the group the Club of Rome would provide endless material for those who believe that the world is controlled by a secret cabal of leaders.

24. John Maddox, *The Doomsday Syndrome: An Attack on Pessimism* (New York: McGraw Hill, 1972). I joined *Nature* in 1995, shortly before Maddox retired as editor. He encouraged my interest in writing about science policy in Pakistan.

25. H. S. D. Cole, Christopher Freeman, Marie Jahoda, and K. L. R. Pavitt, *Models of Doom: A Critique of the Limits to Growth* (New York: Universe Books, 1973). The book was published in Britain under a more academic-sounding title: *Thinking About the Future.*

26. Donella H. Meadows, Dennis L. Meadows, Jørgen Randers, and William W. Behrens III, "A Response to Sussex," in Cole, Freeman, Jahoda, and Pavitt, *Models of Doom,* 221, 236.

27. All of Barbara Ward's quotes are from Ward, "Only One Earth," 20–24.

28. Zuckerman, "Science, Technology and Environmental Management," 129–139.

29. Aurelio Peccei, "Human Settlements," in Strong, *Who Speaks for Earth?,* 154–155. Peccei's lecture was only tangentially about housing or settlements and was mostly a defense of *The Limits to Growth* and the work of the Club of Rome.

30. Maurice Strong's BBC interview from the Stockholm conference is available to view at https://www.youtube.com/watch?v=1YCatox0Lxo, accessed August 19, 2015.

31. Maurice Strong, interview with the author, Geneva, 2009.

32. Parts of the speech are reproduced in Indira Gandhi, *Safeguarding Environment* (New Delhi: Indira Gandhi Memorial Trust, 1992), 17.

SEVEN: "AS VULGAR AS GDP"

1. The inability of Europe and America to give up some of their control over multilateral institutions is cited as a reason why China went ahead in 2015 to create an analog to the World Bank, the Asian Infrastructure Investment Bank.

2. Bill Draper, telephone interview with the author, May 2013.

3. Craig N. Murphy, "Bottoms Up Development Helps Make UNDP a Mammal," in *The United Nations Development Programme: A Better Way?* (Cambridge: Cambridge University Press/UNDP, 2006), 234. Murphy, UNDP's official historian, quotes an interview with Draper, who told him, "It must have been disconcerting to many staffers to have an Administrator dedicated and passionate about the private sector."

4. Sir Richard Jolly, email communication with the author, November 30, and December 2, 2015. In a separate email dated December 4, 2015, Bill Draper also confirmed the lunch with Mahbub ul Haq and General Zia on August 17, 1988, the day of Zia's death.

5. Bill Draper, telephone interview with the author, May 2013.

6. Mahbub ul Haq, "The Birth of the Human Development Index," in *Reflections on Human Development* (New York: Oxford University Press, 1995), 46.

7. Bill Draper also tells his story of meeting Mahbub ul Haq and publishing the Human Development Index in his memoir, William H. Draper III, *The Startup Game: Inside the Partnership Between Venture Capitalists and Entrepreneurs* (New York: Palgrave Macmillan, 2011), 121.

8. Amartya Sen, "The Possibility of Social Choice" (Nobel Lecture, December 8, 1998), accessed August 19, 2015, http://www.nobelprize.org/nobel_prizes/economic-sciences/laureates/1998/sen-lecture.pdf.

9. "A 20th Anniversary Human Development Discussion with Amartya Sen," interview by UNDP for the Human

Development Report 2010, accessed August 19, 2015, https://vimeo.com/16439165.

10. Frances Stewart, interview with the author, July 30, 2014, London.

11. Bill Draper, telephone interview with the author, May 2013.

12. *Human Development Report* (New York: Oxford University Press/UNDP, 1990), 9, accessed August 19, 2015, http://hdr.undp.org/en/reports/global/hdr1990.

13. I conducted two face-to-face interviews with Sir Richard Jolly at his home in Lewes, Sussex, England, first in June 2013 and again in May 2014.

14. Sir Richard Jolly, email communication with the author, November 30, and December 2, 2015.

15. *Human Development Report 2010: The Real Wealth of Nations* (New York: Palgrave Macmillan/UNDP, 2010), 15, accessed August 19, 2015, http://hdr.undp.org/en/content/human-development-report-2010. With the exception of some extra words in the title, the style of the reports had changed little in twenty years: no images; only text, tables, and graphics.

16. Natalie Day, Ehsan Masood, and James Wilsdon, *A New Golden Age? The Prospects for Science and Innovation in the Islamic World* (London: Royal Society, 2010), 5–10.

17. Khadija Haq and Richard Ponzio, *Pioneering the Human Development Revolution: An Intellectual Biography of Mahbub ul Haq* (New Delhi: Oxford University Press, 2008), 3.

18. Ibid.

19. Sir Richard Jolly, interview with the author, Lewes, West Sussex, June 2014.

20. Paul Streeten in the Foreword to Haq, *Reflections on Human Development*, viii. Streeten also writes that Haq was open to changing his mind based on new evidence. He had a plaque on the wall of his World Bank office which said: "It's too late to agree

with me; I've changed my mind." Haq, according to Streeten, gave the plaque to Maurice Strong.

21. *Human Development Report* 1991 (New York: Oxford University Press, 1991), 1.

22. Ben Santer, Tom Wigley, T. M. L. Wigley, T. C. Johns, P. D. Jones, D. J. Karoly, J. F. B. Mitchell, et al., "A Search for Human Influences on the Thermal Structure of the Atmosphere," *Nature*, July 4, 1996, 39–46.

23. Paul Ekins, "The Kuznets curve for the environment and economic growth: examining the evidence," *Environment and Planning A* 29, no. 5 (1997): 805-830.

EIGHT: EXPORTING SHANGRI-LA

1. The actual text of the speech I have so far not been able to locate. But many Bhutanese researchers and policy makers have confirmed that the King did give a speech saying Gross National Happiness is more important than Gross National Product. There are, moreover, numerous references to it in the scholarly literature, including the *Journal of Bhutan Studies*.

2. Following the introduction of Gross National Happiness, the OECD, one of the incubators of the original GDP idea, created an initiative known as the Better Life Index. The World Bank created its own project, which it called WAVES, or Wealth Accounting and the Valuation of Ecosystem Services. These attempts at quantifying nonmonetary indicators, one of the OECD's senior officials told me, were partly to acknowledge to the outside world that the OECD could see problems in GDP, and also to help jump-start an internal conversation among the organization's own economists. Although both the World Bank and the OECD are among the bodies that set the rules for GDP, it seems to me that both WAVES and the Better Life Index are at best marginal to the real game in town.

3.   Brian Groombridge and Martin Jenkins, *World Atlas of Biodiversity: Earth's Living Resources in the 21st Century* (Oakland: University of California Press, 2002), 272–273. Bhutan has 5,603 species of plants, 667 bird species, 200 mammal species, and 49 species of freshwater fish. The country is also home to snow leopards and Bengal tigers, Asian elephants and the exotic and rare black-necked crane.

4.   Ida Kubiszewski, Robert Costanza, Lham Dorji, Philip Thoennes, and Kuenga Tshering, "An Initial Estimate of the Value of Ecosystem Services in Bhutan," *Ecosytem Services* 3 (2013): 11–21.

5.   Ashi Dorji Wangmo Wangchuck, *Treasures of the Thunder Dragon: A Portrait of Bhutan* (New Delhi: Viking/Penguin, 2012), 36–37.

6.   *Statistical Yearbook of Bhutan: 2014* (Thimpu: National Statistics Bureau, Royal Government of Bhutan, 2014). Unless otherwise referenced, the data in this chapter on Bhutan's public sector is from this source.

7.   Health care data in this paragraph is from Chencho Dorji, "Bhutanese Health Care Reform: A Paradigm Shift in Health Care to Increase Gross National Happiness," in *Gross National Happiness: Practice and Measurement: The Proceedings of the Fourth International Conference on Gross National Happiness, 24–26 November 2008*, ed. Dasho Karma Ura and Dorji Penjore (Thimpu: Centre for Bhutan Studies, 2009), 413, accessed October 1, 2015, http://www.bhutanstudies.org.bt/category/conference-proceedings/.

8.   Dasho Karma Ura, Skype interview with the author, December 27, 2013.

9.   Tashi Wangyal, "Rhetoric and Reality: An Assessment of the Impact of WTO on Bhutan," in *The Spider and the Piglet: Proceedings of the First International Seminar on Bhutan Studies*, ed. Karma Ura and Sonam Kinga (Thimpu: Centre for Bhutan

Studies, 2004), accessed October 2, 2015, http://www. bhutanstudies.org.bt/category/conference-proceedings/. The author also makes the point that WTO membership would have an impact on Bhutan's dependence on India, its largest trading partner.

10.   Although the Accelerating Bhutan's Socio-Economic Development project was eventually terminated, Bhutan's government has kept the project website live on its servers (http://www.gnhc.gov.bt/absd/?page_id=25, accessed October 2, 2015). This is an unusual but very welcome step. Often in the public sector records of failed (even completed) projects are quickly removed from the Internet.

11.   In some ways I would say that Bhutan's experience with McKinsey wasn't wholly negative and that people and policy makers both learned some valuable lessons. They discovered that it is entirely possible to question the advice they were getting and to believe that they had something good that they wished to protect. At the same time, they gained experience in handling a major consulting firm, which is an essential skill for any policy maker today.

12.   Gus O'Donnell, Angus Deaton, Martine Durand, David Halpern, and Richard Layard, *Wellbeing and Policy*, Report of the Commission on Wellbeing and Policy (London: Legatum Institute, 2014), accessed October 2, 2015, http://li.com/docs/default-source/commission-on-wellbeing-and-policy/commission-on-wellbeing-and-policy-report---march-2014-pdf.pdf.

13.   Madeline Drexler, *A Splendid Isolation: Lessons on Happiness from the Kingdom of Bhutan* (published by the author, May 2014).

NINE: $33 TRILLION MAN

1.   Herman Daly, "The Canary Has Fallen Silent," *New York Times*, October 14, 1970, 47.

2. Herman Daly told me in an interview on September 5, 2013 that he and Aurelio Peccei never met. That is unfortunate, more so because in 1972–1973 they both, independently, came to the conclusion that growth cannot go on forever; also because they were both engaged in highly public battles with more powerful individuals and institutions. They would have benefited from joining forces.

3. Herman Daly, telephone interview with the author, September 5, 2013.

4. Robert Costanza and Ida Kubiszewski, "The Authorship Structure of Ecosystem Services as a Transdisciplinary Field of Scholarship," *Ecosystem Services* 1 (2012): 16–25.

5. The founding members of ecological economics also include AnnMari Jansson and Joan Martinez-Alier. Cited in Inga Røpke, "The Early History of Modern Ecological Economics," *Ecological Economics* 50 (2004): 293–314.

6. Robert Costanza, Ralph d'Arge, Rudolf de Groot, Stephen Farber, Monica Grasso, Bruce Hannon, Karin Limburg, et al., "The Value of the World's Ecosystem Services and Natural Capital," *Nature* 387 (1997): 253–260.

7. Ibid., 259.

8. *Payment for Ecosystem Services: A Best Practice Guide* (London: Department for Environment, Food and Rural Affairs, May 2013), 11, accessed August 29, 2015, https://www.gov.uk/government/uploads/system/uploads/attachment_data/file/200901/pb13932a-pes-bestpractice-annexa-20130522.pdf.

9. Quoted in William K. Stevens, "What Is Nature Worth? For You, $33 Trillion," *New York Times*, May 20, 1997.

10. Stephen Smith, "David Pearce: Environmental Economist Whose Market-Based Ideas Caught the Changing Tide of the 1980s," *Guardian*, September 22, 2005, accessed August 30, 2015, http://www.theguardian.com/science/2005/sep/22/

highereducation.guardianobituaries. Pearce was an adviser to two successive Conservative ministers of environment in the administration of Margaret Thatcher: Christopher Patten and Michael Heseltine.

11. David Pearce, "Auditing the Earth," *Environment* 40, no. 2 (March 1998): 23–28, accessed August 30, 2015, ftp://131.252.97.79/Transfer/ES_Pubs/ESVal/es_val_critiques/pearce_1998_AuditingTheEarth_Env_v40_2_p23.pdf.

12. Costanza and his team worked out the cultural value of oceans to be $76 per hectare as the difference between the values of coastal and noncoastal property. This was on the basis that people would pay more to live near an ocean, reflecting the increased cultural value of such places.

13. Pearce, "Auditing the Earth," 26.

14. Robert Costanza, telephone interview with the author, May 17, 2013.

15. Robert Costanza, Ralph D'Arge, Rudolf de Groot, Stephen Farber, Monica Grasso, Bruce Hannon, Karin Limburg, et al., "Costanza and His Coauthors Reply," *Environment* 40, no. 2 (March 1998): 26–27.

16. With the benefit of hindsight I do think that the journal panicked into taking a hasty decision and that it could have had more of a discussion with the reviewers before showing Costanza the door. Usually, when a manuscript is sent out to peer review, the journal's editors are confident about its merits. Peer reviewers' role is to suggest ways of improving a text. Their suggestions and criticisms are put to the authors, who are given an opportunity to respond, before possibly another round of peer review. *Science*'s team was clearly so shaken by the extreme reactions, they decided to cut their losses and turned the paper down.

TEN: STERN LESSONS

1. Before that Nicholas Stern had forged a career in development economics, which is the study of how poor countries can become richer. Indeed, his signature work, his long-lived academic achievement, is a social history of a small village in the north of India. For forty years Stern has documented the changing lives of families in the tiny farming village of Palanpur.

2. Tony Blair, *A Journey* (London: Hutchinson/Random House, 2010), 497. Blair had assured Gordon Brown that he would not fight a third election in 2005, allowing Brown to fulfill his ambition to become prime minister. However, Blair did not honor this commitment, he says, on the grounds that Brown was insufficiently committed to Blair's public service reform agenda.

3. Nicholas Stern, telephone interview with the author, June 19, 2014. One of the commission's more innovative ideas was to invite Africa's leaders to temporarily leave the comfort of their chauffeur-driven cars and embark on a roadshow the length and breadth of the continent. Stern and his team invited thousands of students, farmers, industrialists, campaigners, and many others and arranged for them to attend public meetings where heads of state would be present. I attended one such event in Egypt's port city Alexandria and I can remember all too well how the (mostly young) audience was both shocked and impressed that their continent's usually aloof leadership had not only bothered to turn up, but had come to listen and not to lecture.

4. Tony Blair and the Commission for Africa, *Our Common Interest: Report of the Commission for Africa* (Commission for Africa, March 2005). Although the author list was headed by Tony Blair, much of the actual drafting was done by Stern and his team at the Commission for Africa Secretariat in London.

5.   The UK's Climate Change Act of 2008 mandates 80 percent reductions in emissions of greenhouse gases by 2050.

6.   The UK's first secretary of state for energy and climate change was Ed Miliband, who would later succeed Gordon Brown as leader of the Labour Party from 2010 to 2015.

7.   Under Michael Meacher's tenure, the environment lobby had a direct line to government. One of their collective achievements was to oppose plans from scientists or farmers for genetically modified crops to be grown on a commercial scale, as Meacher told me in an interview for a BBC Radio documentary. Ehsan Masood, "Science: Right or Left?" BBC Radio 4, broadcast August 11, 2013, accessed August 30, 2015, http://www.bbc.co.uk/programmes/b037tsw0.

8.   Croatia had not yet become a member of the European Union.

9.   The UK's priorities for the EU presidency included budgetary matters as well as the prospect of Turkey's accession, which at the time was a serious prospect.

10.   Blair, *A Journey*, 557.

11.   Nicholas Stern, *The Economics of Climate Change: The Stern Review* (Cambridge: Cambridge University Press, 2007).

12.   Nicholas Stern, telephone interview with the author, June 19, 2014.

13.   At the time of the Stern review, the UK Foreign Office, the British Council, and the World Service of the BBC had been signed up to a UK government initiative called the Public Diplomacy Board. The idea was to pool their resources on activities that would create favorable impressions of the UK among international audiences. The board has since been disbanded.

14.   I remember this meeting particularly well in part because my plane had landed in the middle of the night on a flight where I was the only passenger.

15.   My dispatches from the African Union heads of government meeting in January 2007 are archived at "In the Field,"

Nature.com, accessed August 30, 2015, http://blogs.nature.com/inthefield/author/emasood.

16. Masood, "Science: Right or Left?"

ELEVEN: "NOTHING IS MORE DESTRUCTIVE OF DEMOCRACY"

1. Joseph Stiglitz, Amartya Sen, and Jean-Paul Fitoussi, *Mismeasuring Our Lives: Why GDP Doesn't Add Up: The Report of the Commission on the Measurement of Economic Performance and Social Progress* (New York: New Press, 2010), viii.

2. The Sarkozy commission team would also include Nicholas Stern.

3. Stiglitz, Sen and Fitoussi, *Mismeasuring Our Lives*, 10–18.

EPILOGUE: UNFINISHED REVOLUTION

1. Robin Harding, "Data Shift to Lift US Economy by 3%," *Financial Times*, April 21, 2013.

2. Ben Martin, "The Economic Benefits of Publicly-Funded Research: A Critical Review," *Research Policy* 30 (2001): 509–532. The economist Ben Martin, professor at the Science Policy Research Unit at the University of Sussex, has spent the better part of a professional lifetime understanding the links between science and growth. He says there is no straightforward or linear relationship.

3. Fernando Galindo-Rueda, "Developing an R&D Satellite Account for the UK: A Preliminary Analysis," *Economic and Labour Market Review* 1, no. 12 (December 2007): 18–29, accessed October 4, 2015, http://www.ons.gov.uk/ons/rel/elmr/economic-and-labour-market-review/no--12--december-2007/developing-an-r-d-satellite-account-for-the-uk--a-preliminary-analysis.pdf. At the end of 2007, the UK's Office for National Statistics forecast that recapitalizing R&D in the national accounts would raise levels of UK GDP by 1.5 percent.

4. Alexander King, *Let the Cat Turn Around: One Man's Traverse of the Twentieth Century* (London: CPTM Publishing, 2006), 236–249. King devotes an entire chapter of his memoir to his efforts to persuade ministers and heads of government that science spending must be seen as an investment toward economic growth. He recalls one encounter with the education minister of the Netherlands, who likened such an idea to "prostitution of science." In his later years, King, too, would come around to that view.

5. Benoit Godin, "The Making of Statistical Standards: The OECD and the Frascati Manual, 1962–2002" (Working Paper 39, Project on the History and Sociology of STI Statistics, 2008), 34, accessed October 4, 2015, http://www.csiic.ca/PDF/Godin_39.pdf.

6. Ibid., 17.

7. Fernando Galinda-Rueda, "Towards R&D Capitalisation: An OECD Perspective," OECD Directorate for Science, Technology and Industry, Economic Analysis and Statistics Division (London, April 2011), 3–4, accessed October 4, 2015, https://community.oecd.org/docs/DOC-41735.

8. Murat Tanriseven, Dirk van den Bergen, Myriam van Rooijen-Horsten, and Mark de Haan, *Research and Development Statistics: R&D Capitalisation in the Knowledge Module* (The Hague: Statistics Netherlands, 2008), 14–15, accessed October 4, 2015, http://www.cbs.nl/NR/rdonlyres/9F8B7800-9261-4ECD-9664-E5F00880CCEE/0/200801x41pub.pdf. In this paper, published by the Netherlands' office for national statistics, an expert advisory group to the government is reported to have recommended that freely available scientific knowledge should not be moved into the investment column of GDP.

THE END OF THE WORD: A NOTE ON SYMBOLS

1. Felix Salmon, "The Secret Formula That Destroyed Wall Street: How One Simple Equation Made Billions for Bankers—and Nuked Your 401(k)," *Wired*, March 2009, 74–85.

2. Joseph Mazur, *Englightening Symbols: A Short History of Mathematical Notation and Its Hidden Powers* (Princeton, NJ: Princeton University Press, 2014, 85–92.

3. Ibid., after p. 80.

4. Roy Harrod, *The Life of John Maynard Keynes* (New York: W. W. Norton, 1951), 624–625.

5. Paul Krugman, "How Did Economists Get It So Wrong?" *New York Times Magazine*, September 2, 2009, accessed October 4, 2015, http://www.nytimes.com/2009/09/06/magazine/06Economic-t.html?em=&pagewanted=all.

6. E. O. Wilson, "Great Scientist ≠ Good at Math," *Wall Street Journal*, April 5, 2013, accessed October 4, 2013, http://www.wsj.com/articles/SB100014241278873236116045 78398943650327184.

BIBLIOGRAPHY

LIBRARIES AND ARCHIVES

Archives of the Massachusetts Institute of Technology, Cambridge, Massachusetts.

Library of the Institute of Development Studies, University of Sussex, Falmer, Sussex.

Marshall Economics Library, University of Cambridge.

MIT Museum, Cambridge, Massachusetts.

National Archives and Records Administration, Washington DC.

Pakistan Management Association Library, Karachi.

BOOKS AND THESES

Tariq Ali, *Can Pakistan Survive? The Death of a State* (New York: Penguin, 1983).

Vincent Bevins, *The Jakarta Method: Washington's Anticommunist Crusade & the Mass Murder Program that Shaped Our World* (New York: Public Affairs, 2020).

Donald L. M. Blackmer and Max Millikan, *The Emerging Nations: Their Growth and United States Policy* (eds) (London: Asia Publishing House, 1962).

Donald L. M. Blackmer, *The MIT Center for International Studies: The Founding Years, 1951–1969* (Cambridge, MA: MIT Center for International Studies, 2002).

Tony Blair, *A Journey* (London: Hutchinson/Random House, 2010).

John Bresnan, *At Home Abroad: The Ford Foundation in Indonesia 1953–1973* (Jakarta: Equinox, 2006).

Andrew Brown, *Fishing in Utopia: Sweden and the Future That Disappeared* (London: Granta, 2009).

Rachel Carson, *Silent Spring* (Houghton Mifflin, 1962).

Colin Clark, *The National Income 1924–1931* (London: Macmillan, 1932).

Colin Clark, *National Income and Outlay* (London: Macmillan, 1937).

H. S. D. Cole, Christopher Freeman, Marie Jahoda, and K. L. R. Pavitt, *Models of Doom: A Critique of the Limits to Growth* (New York: Universe Books, 1973).

Giovanni Andrea Cornia, Richard Jolly, Frances Stewart, *Adjustment with a Human Face: Protecting the Vulnerable and Promoting Growth* (Oxford: Oxford University Press, 1987).

Diane Coyle, *GDP: A Brief but Affectionate History* (Princeton, NJ: Princeton University Press, 2013).

Herman Daly, *Steady State Economics* (San Francisco: W. H. Freeman and Company, 1977)

William H. Draper III, *The Startup Game: Inside the Partnership Between Venture Capitalists and Entrepreneurs* (New York: Palgrave Macmillan, 2011).

Madeline Drexler, *A Splendid Isolation: Lessons on Happiness from the Kingdom of Bhutan* (published by the author, May 2014).

Lorenzo Fioramonti, *The World After GDP* (London: Polity Press, 2017).

John Kenneth Galbraith, *A History of Economics: The Past as the Present* (London: Penguin Books, 1987).

Jean Gartlan, *Barbara Ward: Her Life and Letters* (New York: Continuum International Publishing Group, 2010)

Brian Groombridge and Martin Jenkins, *World Atlas of Biodiversity: Earth's Living Resources in the 21st Century* (Oakland: University of California Press, 2002).

David Halberstam, *The Best and the Brightest* (New York: Ballantyne Books, 1992; originally published 1969).

Khadija Haq and Richard Ponzio, *Pioneering the Human Development Revolution: An Intellectual Biography of Mahbub ul Haq* (New Delhi: Oxford University Press, 2008).

Mahbub ul Haq, *The Strategy of Economic Planning: Case Study of Pakistan* (Oxford: Oxford University Press, 1966).

Mahbub ul Haq, *The Poverty Curtain: Choices for the Third World* (New York: Columbia University Press, 1976).

Mahbub ul Haq, *Reflections on Human Development* (New York: Oxford University Press, 1995).

John P. Hardt and Vladimir G. Treml, *Soviet Economic Statistics* (Durham, NC: Duke University Press, 1972).

John P. Hardt, Marvin Hoffenberg, Norman Kaplan, Herbert S. Levine (eds), *Mathematics and Computers in Soviet Economic Planning* (New Haven, CT: Yale University Press, 1967).

Roy Harrod, *The Life of John Maynard Keynes* (New York: W. W. Norton, 1951).

Jonathan Haskel and Stian Westlake, *Capitalism Without Capital: The Rise of the Intangible Economy* (Princeton, NJ: Princeton University Press, 2018).

Rutger Hoekstra, *Replacing GDP by 2030* (Cambridge, Cambridge University Press, 2019).

Stanley Johnson, *UNEP: The First 40 Years* (Nairobi: UNEP Publishing, 2012).

John Maynard Keynes, *The Economic Consequences of the Peace* (New York: Harcourt Brace Jovanovich, 1920).

John Maynard Keynes, *The General Theory of Employment, Interest and Money* (New York: Harcourt, Brace & World, 1936).

John Maynard Keynes, *How to Pay for the War* (London: Macmillan, 1940).

Nikita S. Khrushchev, *Let us Live in Peace and Friendship: The Visit of N. S. Khrushchev to the United States* (New York: Crosscurrents Press, 1960).

Alexander King, *Let the Cat Turn Around: One Man's Traverse of the Twentieth Century* (London: CPTM Publishing, 2006).

Philip Lepenies, *The Power of a Single Number: A Political History of GDP* (New York: Columbia University Press, 2016).

Angus Maddison, *Class Structure and Economic Growth: India and Pakistan Since the Moghuls* (London: George Allen and Unwin, 1971).

John Maddox, *The Doomsday Syndrome: An Attack on Pessimism* (New York: McGraw Hill, 1972).

Mariana Mazzucato, *The Entrepreneurial State* (London: Anthem Press, 2013).

Mariana Mazzucato, *The Value of Everything: Making and Taking in the Global Economy* (London: Penguin, 2019).

Donella H. Meadows, Dennis L. Meadows, Jørgen Randers, William W. Behrens III, *The Limits to Growth* (London: Pan Books, 1972).

David Milne, *America's Rasputin: Walt Rostow and the Vietnam War* (New York: Hill & Wang, 2008).

Benjamin Mitra-Kahn, "Redefining the Economy: How the 'Economy' Was Invented in 1620 and Has Been Redefined Ever Since" (doctoral thesis, City University London, 2011).

Jeffrey Z. Muller, *The Tyranny of Metrics* (Princeton, NJ: Princeton University Press, 2019).

Craig N. Murphy, "Bottoms Up Development Helps Make UNDP a Mammal," in *The United Nations Development Programme: A Better Way?* (Cambridge: Cambridge University Press/UNDP, 2006).

Gustav Papanek, *Pakistan's Development: Social Goals and Private Incentives* (Cambridge, MA: Harvard University Press, 1967).

Gustav F. Papanek (ed.), *The Indonesian Economy* (New York: Praeger, 1980).

Dirk Philipsen, *The Little Big Number: How GDP Came to Rule the World and What to Do About It* (Princeton, NJ: Princeton University Press, 2015).

David Pilling, *The Growth Delusion: The Wealth and Well-Being of Nations* (London: Bloomsbury, 2018).

Kate Raworth, *Doughnut Economics: Seven Ways to Think Like a 21st-Century Economist* (London: Random House, 2017).

W. W. Rostow (ed.), *The Economics of Take-Off Into Sustained Growth* (New York: St Martin's Press, 1963).

W. W. Rostow, *The Stages of Economic Growth: A Non-Communist Manifesto* (Cambridge: Cambridge University Press, 1960).

W. W. Rostow, *The Dynamics of Soviet Society* (London: Secker & Warburg, 1953).

W. W. Rostow, *The British Economy of the Nineteenth Century* (Oxford: Oxford University Press, 1948).

W. W. Rostow, *The Process of Economic Growth* (New York: Norton, 1952).

W. W. Rostow, *The Process of Economic Growth* (London: Oxford University Press, 1960).

Matthias Schmelzer, *The Hegemony of Growth: The OECD and the Making of the Economic Growth Paradigm* (Cambridge: Cambridge University Press, 2015).

Ellen W. Schrecker, *No Ivory Tower: McCarthyism and the Universities* (Oxford: Oxford University Press, 1988).

Robert Skidelsky, *John Maynard Keynes: The Economist as Saviour 1920–1937* (London: Macmillan, 1992).

Josiah Stamp, *Wealth and Taxable Capacity: The Newmarch Lectures for 1920–1 on Current and Statistical Problems in Wealth and Industry* (London: P. S. King & Son, 1922).

Nicholas Stern, *The Economics of Climate Change: The Stern Review* (Cambridge: Cambridge University Press, 2007).

Joseph Stiglitz, Amartya Sen, and Jean-Paul Fitoussi, *Mismeasuring Our Lives: Why GDP Doesn't Add Up: The Report of the Commission on the Measurement of Economic Performance and Social Progress* (New York: New Press, 2010).

Maurice Strong (edited), *Who Speaks for Earth?* (New York: W. W. Norton and Co., 1972).

Maurice Strong, *Where on Earth Are We Going?* (New York: Texere Publishing, 2000).

Ashi Dorji Wangmo Wangchuck, *Treasures of the Thunder Dragon: A Portrait of Bhutan* (New Delhi: Viking/Penguin, 2012).

Michael Ward, *Quantifying the World: UN Ideas and Statistics* (Bloomington: Indiana University Press/United Nations Intellectual History Project, 2000)

RESEARCH PAPERS, REPORTS, SPEECHES AND MEDIA ARTICLES

Charles Bean, "Independent Review of UK Economic Statistics: Interim Report," HM Treasury, December 2, 2015, accessed December 8, 2015, https://www.gov.uk/government/publications/independent-review-of-uk-economic-statistics-interim-report.

Ragna Boden, "Cold War Economics: Soviet Aid to Indonesia," *Journal of Cold War Studies* 10, 3 (2008).

Mauro Boianovsky and Kevin D. Hoover, "In the Kingdom of Solovia: The Rise of Growth Economists at MIT, 1956–70," *History of Political Economy* 46 (2014).

W. Robert Brazelton, "The Economics of Leon Hirsch Keyserling," *Journal of Economic Perspectives* 11, 4 (1997).

Gordon Brown, "Budget Statement," *Hansard Parliamentary Debates*, Commons, April 9, 2003, accessed July 31, 2015, http://www.publications.parliament.uk/pa/cm200203/cmhansrd/vo030409/debtext/30409-04.htm.

Carol S. Carson, "The History of the United States National Income and Product Accounts," *Review of Income and Wealth 21* (1975): 153–181.

Rachel Carson, "Silent Spring," *The New Yorker*, June 16, 1962, 35.

Robert Costanza, Ralph d'Arge, Rudolf de Groot, Stephen Farber, Monica Grasso, Bruce Hannon, Karin Limburg, et al., "The Value of the World's Ecosystem Services and Natural Capital," *Nature* 387 (1997): 253–260.

Robert Costanza and Ida Kubiszewski, "The Authorship Structure of Ecosystem Services as a Transdisciplinary Field of Scholarship," *Ecosystem Services* 1 (2012): 16–25.

Robert Costanza, Ralph D'Arge, Rudolf de Groot, Stephen Farber, Monica Grasso, Bruce Hannnon, Karin Limburg, et al., "Costanza and His Coauthors Reply," *Environment* 40, no. 2 (March 1998): 26–27.

Diane Coyle and Benjamin Mitra-Kahn, *Making the Future Count*, Indigo Prize-winning essay, 2017, accessed December 12, 2020, http://global-perspectives.org.uk/wp-content/uploads/2017/10/making-the-future-count.pdf.

G. Daily, J. Liu, Z. Ouyang et al, "Using Gross Ecosystem Product to Value Nature in Decision-Making," *Proceedings of the National*

Academy of Sciences 117 (2020), 14593–14601, accessed December 12, 2020, https://doi.org/10.1073/pnas.1911439117.

Biplab Dasgupta and Dudley Seers, "Statistical Policy in Less Developed Countries" (report of the conference Statistical Policy in Less Developed Countries, Institute of Development Studies, University of Sussex, May 12–16, 1975).

Natalie Day, Ehsan Masood, and James Wilsdon, *A New Golden Age? The Prospects for Science and Innovation in the Islamic World* (London: Royal Society, 2010).

Carmen DeNavas-Walt and Bernadette D. Proctor, "Income and Poverty in the United States: 2013," US Census Bureau, September 2014, accessed August 1, 2015, http://www.census.gov/content/dam/Census/library/publications/2014/demo/p60-249.pdf.

William Dalrymple, "On the Trail of the White Mughals," *Daily Telegraph*, August 29, 2015.

Herman Daly, "The Canary Has Fallen Silent," *New York Times*, October 14, 1970, 47.

Chencho Dorji, "Bhutanese Health Care Reform: A Paradigm Shift in Health Care to Increase Gross National Happiness," in *Gross National Happiness: Practice and Measurement: The Proceedings of the Fourth International Conference on Gross National Happiness, 24–26 November 2008*, ed. Dasho Karma Ura and Dorji Penjore (Thimpu: Centre for Bhutan Studies, 2009), 413, accessed October 1, 2015, http://www.bhutanstudies.org.bt/category/conference-proceedings/.

Economy of Pakistan (Karachi: Office of the Economic Adviser, Ministry of Economic Affairs, Government of Pakistan, 1950), 333–340.

Fernando Galindo-Rueda, "Developing an R&D Satellite Account for the UK: A Preliminary Analysis," *Economic and Labour Market Review* 1, no. 12 (December 2007): 18–29, accessed October 4, 2015, http://www.ons.gov.uk/ons/rel/elmr/economic-and-labour-market-review/no--12--december-2007/developing-an-r-d-satellite-account-for-the-uk--a-preliminary-analysis.pdf.

Fernando Galinda-Rueda, "Towards R&D Capitalisation: An OECD Perspective," OECD Directorate for Science, Technology and Industry, Economic Analysis and Statistics Division (London, April

2011), 3–4, accessed October 4, 2015, https://community.oecd.org/docs/DOC-41735.

"GDP: One of the Great Inventions of the 20th Century," *Survey of Current Business*, Bureau of Economic Analysis, January 2000.

Benoit Godin, "The Making of Statistical Standards: The OECD and the Frascati Manual, 1962–2002" (Working Paper 39, Project on the History and Sociology of STI Statistics, 2008), 34, accessed October 4, 2015, http://www.csiic.ca/PDF/Godin_39.pdf.

"Gross Domestic Product: Preliminary Estimate, Q2 2012," Office for National Statistics, July 25, 2012, accessed July 31, 2015, http://www.ons.gov.uk/ons/rel/gva/gross-domestic-product--preliminary-estimate/q2-2012/index.html.

Mahbub ul Haq, "A Critical Review of the Third Five Year Plan," *Management and National Growth: Proceedings of the Management Convention Held at Karachi*, April 24–25, 1968, 23–33.

Robin Harding, "Data Shift to Lift US Economy by 3%," *Financial Times*, April 21, 2013.

Roy Harrod, "Wealth of Nations," *Financial Times*, April 12, 1960.

Benjamin Higgins, "The Indonesia Five-Year Plan: Proposals for Research," MIT Center for International Studies, September 6, 1957.

Human Development Report (New York: Oxford University Press/UNDP, 1990), 9, accessed August 19, 2015, http://hdr.undp.org/en/reports/global/hdr1990.

Human Development Report 2010: The Real Wealth of Nations (New York: Palgrave Macmillan/UNDP, 2010), 15, accessed August 19, 2015, http://hdr.undp.org/en/content/human-development-report-2010.

The Human Environment: The British View, Report Prepared on the Occasion of the Stockholm Conference on the Human Environment (London: Her Majesty's Stationery Office, 1972).

Zahid Hussain, "The First Five Year Plan: Size, Objectives and Limitations," *Pakistan Economic and Social Review* 5 (1956): 3, accessed August 17, 2015, http://pu.edu.pk/home/journal/7/Volume_5_No_1_1956.html.

"In the Name of GDP: In China, a TV soap on corruption attracts a mass following," *The Economist*, May 13, 2017.

Wang Jinnan, "Revive China's Green GDP Programme," *Nature* 534, 37 (2016), accessed December 12, 2020, https://www.nature.com/articles/534037b.

Paul Krugman, "How Did Economists Get It So Wrong?" *New York Times Magazine*, September 2, 2009, accessed October 4, 2015, http://www.nytimes.com/2009/09/06/magazine/06Economic-t.html?em=&pagewanted=all.

Ida Kubiszewski, Robert Costanza, Lham Dorji, Philip Thoennes, and Kuenga Tshering, "An Initial Estimate of the Value of Ecosystem Services in Bhutan," *Ecosytem Services* (2012).

Max Lerner, "Takeoff Road," *New York Post*, November 21, 1960.

"Labour Market Statistics, August 2012," Office for National Statistics, accessed July 31, 2015, http://www.ons.gov.uk/ons/rel/lms/labour-market-statistics/august-2012/index.html.

Jan Luiten van Zanden, Joerg Baten, Marco Mira d'Ercole, Auke Rijpma, Conal Smith and Marcel Timmer *How Was Life: Global Well-Being Since 1820* (Paris: OECD Publishing, 2014).

Russell Lynch, "Work Experience Chancellor George Osborne Urged to Quit as GDP Slumps," *Independent*, July 26, 2010, accessed July 31, 2015, http://www.independent.co.uk/news/uk/politics/work-experience-chancellor-george-osborne-urged-to-quit-as-gdp-slumps-7976829.html.

Ben Martin, "The Economic Benefits of Publicly-Funded Research: A Critical Review," *Research Policy* 30 (2001): 509–532.

Ehsan Masood, "In the Field," Dispatches from the African Union Summit 2007, accessed August 30, 2015, http://blogs.nature.com/inthefield/author/emasood.

Ehsan Masood, "The Globe's Green Avenger," *Nature*, July 22, 2009, 454–455.

Ehsan Masood, "Science: Right or Left?" BBC Radio 4, broadcast August 11, 2013, accessed August 30, 2015, http://www.bbc.co.uk/programmes/b037tsw0.

Joseph Mazur, *Enlightening Symbols: A Short History of Mathematical Notation and Its Hidden Powers* (Princeton, NJ: Princeton University Press, 2014.

Donella H. Meadows, Dennis L. Meadows, Jørgen Randers, and William W. Behrens III, "A Response to Sussex," in Cole, Freeman, Jahoda, and Pavitt, *Models of Doom*.

Walter Millis, "How to Compete with the Russians," *The New York Times*, February 2, 1958.

David Moss and Joseph P. Gownder, "The Origins of National Income Accounting," *Harvard Business Review*, December 30, 1998.

National Income 1929–32, Department of Commerce, in response to Senate Resolution No. 220, 72nd Congress (Washington, DC: Government Printing Office, 1934).

Gus O'Donnell, Angus Deaton, Martine Durand, David Halpern, and Richard Layard, *Wellbeing and Policy*, Report of the Commission on Wellbeing and Policy (London: Legatum Institute, 2014), accessed October 2, 2015, http://li.com/docs/default-source/commission-on-wellbeing-and-policy/commission-on-wellbeing-and-policy-report---march-2014-pdf.pdf.

Our Common Interest: Report of the Commission for Africa (Commission for Africa, March 2005).

Gustav Papanek, "The Development Miracle" (speech under the joint auspices of the Pakistani-American Chambers of Commerce and the Asia Society, New York, May 4, 1965).

Payment for Ecosystem Services: A Best Practice Guide (London: Department for Environment, Food and Rural Affairs, May 2013), 11, accessed August 29, 2015, https://www.gov.uk/government/uploads/system/uploads/attachment_data/file/200901/pb13932a-pes-bestpractice-annexa-20130522.pdf.

David Pearce, "Auditing the Earth," *Environment* 40, no. 2 (March 1998): 23–28, accessed August 30, 2015, ftp://131.252.97.79/Transfer/ES_Pubs/ESVal/es_val_critiques/pearce_1998_AuditingTheEarth_Env_v40_2_p23.pdf.

"Rise in Home Movers Drives Boost in House Purchase Loans and Gross Lending," Council of Mortgage Lenders, September 12, 2012, accessed July 31, 2015, http://www.cml.org.uk/news/press-releases/3302/.

Inga Røpke, "The Early History of Modern Ecological Economics," *Ecological Economics* 50 (2004): 293–314.

"Rostow on Growth," *The Economist*, August 15 and August 22, 1959.

W. W. Rostow, "The Stages of Economic Growth and the Problems of Peaceful Co-Existence" can be accessed at: https://dspace.mit.edu/handle/1721.1/83060.

Felix Salmon, "The Secret Formula That Destroyed Wall Street: How One Simple Equation Made Billions for Bankers—and Nuked Your 401(k)," *Wired*, March 2009, 74–85.

B. Santer, T. M. L. Wigley, T. C. Johns, P. D. Jones, D. J. Karoly, J. F. B. Mitchell, et al., "A Search for Human Influences on the Thermal Structure of the Atmosphere," *Nature*, July 4, 1996, 39–46.

Dudley Seers, "What Are We Trying to Measure?" special issue on development indicators, *Journal of Development Studies* 8, no. 3 (April 1972): 21.

Amartya Sen, "The Possibility of Social Choice" (Nobel Lecture, December 8, 1998), accessed August 19, 2015, http://www.nobelprize.org/nobel_prizes/economic-sciences/laureates/1998/sen-lecture.pdf.

Amartya Sen, "A 20th Anniversary Human Development Discussion with Amartya Sen," interview by UNDP for the Human Development Report 2010, accessed August 19, 2015, https://vimeo.com/16439165.

Stephen Smith, "David Pearce: Environmental Economist Whose Market-Based Ideas Caught the Changing Tide of the 1980s," *Guardian*, September 22, 2005, accessed August 30, 2015, http://www.theguardian.com/science/2005/sep/22/highereducation.guardianobituaries.

Statistical Yearbook of Bhutan: 2014 (Thimpu: National Statistics Bureau, Royal Government of Bhutan, 2014).

William K. Stevens, "What Is Nature Worth? For You, $33 Trillion," *New York Times*, May 20, 1997.

Richard Stone, "The National Income, Output and Expenditure of the United States of America," *Economic Journal* 206–207 (1942): 154–175.

Paul Streeten, "Dudley Seers (1920–83): A Personal Appreciation," *IDS Bulletin* 20, no. 3 (July 1989): 26.

Murat Tanriseven, Dirk van den Bergen, Myriam van Rooijen-Horsten, and Mark de Haan, *Research and Development Statistics: R&D Capitalisation in the Knowledge Module* (The Hague: Statistics Netherlands, 2008), 14–15, accessed October 4, 2015, http://www.cbs.nl/NR/rdonlyres/9F8B7800-9261-4ECD-9664-E5F00880CCEE/0/200801x41pub.pdf.

"TARP Programs," US Treasury Department, accessed August 1, 2015, http://www.treasury.gov/initiatives/financial-stability/TARP-Programs/Pages/default.aspx.

"Triumph in Pakistan: Ike and President Ayub," *Life*, December 21, 1959.

United Nations Statistical Commission Report on the 51st session (March 3–6, 2020), Economic and Social Council Official Records, 2020, Supplement No. 4, accessed December 12, 2020, https://unstats.un.org/unsd/statcom/51st-session/documents/2020-37-FinalReport-E.pdf.

Marina Vornovytskyy, Alfred Gottschalck, and Adam Smith, "Household Debt in the US: 2000 to 2011," accessed July 31, 2015, https://www.census.gov/people/wealth/files/Debt%20Highlights%202011.pdf.

Tashi Wangyal, "Rhetoric and Reality: An Assessment of the Impact of WTO on Bhutan," in *The Spider and the Piglet: Proceedings of the First International Seminar on Bhutan Studies*, ed. Karma Ura and Sonam Kinga (Thimpu: Centre for Bhutan Studies, 2004), accessed October 2, 2015, http://www.bhutanstudies.org.bt/category/conference-proceedings/.

Lawrence White, "Industrial Concentration and Industrial Economic Power in Pakistan: The 22 Families (plus a Few More)" (Discussion Paper 24, Research Program in Economic Development, Woodrow Wilson School, Princeton University, July 1972), accessed August 18, 2015, http://www.princeton.edu/rpds/papers/WP_024.pdf.

E. O. Wilson, "Great Scientist ≠ Good at Math," *Wall Street Journal*, April 5, 2013, accessed October 4, 2013, http://www.wsj.com/articles/SB10001424127887323611604578398943650327184.

Yuri Zhukov, "Snipes on a Bog," *Pravda*, October 19, 1959.

INDEX